Nineteen Eighty-Four

Past, Present, and Future

TWAYNE'S MASTERWORK STUDIES
ROBERT LECKER, GENERAL EDITOR

NINETEEN EIGHTY-FOUR

PAST, PRESENT, AND FUTURE

Patrick Reilly

TWAYNE PUBLISHERS
BOSTON

Nineteen Eighty-Four: Past, Present, and Future
Patrick Reilly

Twayne's Masterwork Studies No. 30

Copyright 1989 by G. K. Hall & Co.
All rights reserved.
Published by Twayne Publishers
A division of G. K. Hall & Co.
70 Lincoln Street, Boston, Massachusetts 02111

Copyediting supervised by Barbara Sutton.
Book production by Gabrielle B. McDonald.

Typeset in 10/14 pt. Sabon
by Compset, Inc., of Beverly, Massachusetts

Printed on permanent/durable acid-free paper
and bound in the United States of America

Library of Congress Cataloging–in–Publication Data

Reilly, Patrick.
    Nineteen eighty-four : past, present, and future / Patrick Reilly.
      p.   cm. — (Twayne's masterwork studies ; no. 30)
    Bibliography: p.
    Includes index.
    ISBN 0-8057-8065-3 (alk. paper). — ISBN 0-8057-8110-2 (pbk. :
alk. paper)
    1. Orwell, George, 1903-1950. Nineteen eighty-four. I. Title.
II. Title: 1984. III. Series.
    PR6029.R8N666   1989
823'.912—dc19   88-35225
                                              CIP

For Kevin, Patrick and Joanne

The fact is that every writer *creates* his own precursors. His work modifies our conception of the past, as it will modify the future.
—Jorge Luis Borges,
   Labyrinths

CONTENTS

A NOTE ON THE REFERENCES AND ACKNOWLEDGMENTS

My preeminent obligation is to my wife, Rose, for her patience and skill in preparing the manuscript for publication. I would also like to thank my colleagues, Professor Philip Hobsbaum and Dr. Donald Mackenzie, for their willingness to listen and respond. I am especially grateful to Michael Foot for his generous advice and encouragement.

This study is an extension and elaboration of ideas first advanced in the chapter dealing with *Nineteen Eighty-Four* in my book *George Orwell: The Age's Adversary*, published by the Macmillan Press, London and St. Martin's Press, New York.

I have chosen the Penguin edition of *Nineteen Eighty-Four* (first published in 1954, reprinted twice in 1987) as the most readily available edition of the text. Page references within the study are to this edition.

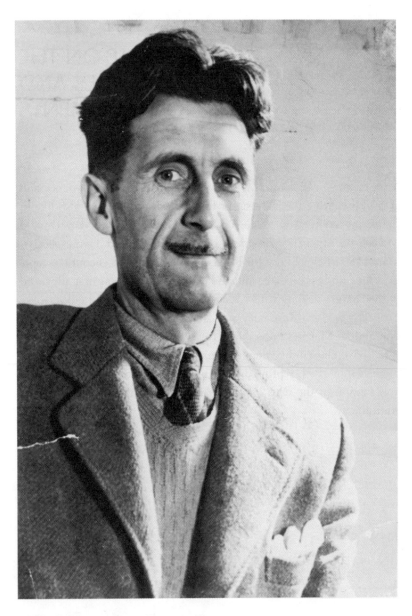

GEORGE ORWELL (ERIC ARTHUR BLAIR)
1903–1950

CHRONOLOGY: GEORGE ORWELL'S LIFE AND WORKS

1903	Eric Arthur Blair born 25 June in Mothari, Bengal, five years after his sister Marjorie, also born in India; son of Richard Walmesley Blair, employed in the Opium Department of the Government of India, and Ida Mabel Limouzin, daughter of a French teak merchant from Moulmein, Burma.
1904	Ida Blair takes her two children back to England to Henley-on-Thames, Oxfordshire, while Richard Blair stays in India. (It was customary for "Anglo-Indians" to bring up their children in England.) Even as a baby Eric shows signs of chest trouble, which is to affect him all his life.
1908	Sent (like sisters Marjorie before him and Avril after him) to a small Anglican convent school in Henley.
1911	Sent to a new but successful preparatory school, St. Cyprian's, Eastbourne, Sussex. As a child of the "lower-upper-middle class" (people not hard up but always pressed for money to live "as they ought"), is taken on by the school at half-fees, for as "scholarship fodder" he could bring credit and further financial success to the school. (He provides a virulent description of the school [bad food, inadequate heating, poor sanitation, cruelty, and snobbery.] in "Such, Such Were the Joys," which was not published for fear of libel until after the death of the school's proprietor in 1967. This account has been challenged by other former pupils, however.) 24 June, "steals" the copy of *Gulliver's Travels* intended as his birthday gift; addicted to Swift, who remains the major literary influence of his life.
1916	Leaves St. Cyprian's.
1917	Spends nine weeks at Wellington College before going to Eton College, famous public school, as a Colleger (a King's Scholar), paying far less than the Oppidans (the great majority of boys

attending the school). He thus belonged to an intellectual elite existing within a social elite. Not an academic success; does not go, or seem to want to go, on to university, although there are obviously financial obstacles.

1921   Leaves Eton.

1922   Joins through open examination the Indian Imperial Police and serves until 1927 as a subdivisional officer in Burma in a life of boredom and bugles. Various postings during which dislike of the service hardens into hatred. Rejects imperialism in the belief that his place was on the other side of the prison bars.

1927   Resigns and returns to England.

1928   Goes to Paris, where he spends about eighteen months, in order to become a writer. As his money runs out, is forced to become a dishwasher in various hotels and restaurants.

1929   Returns to England at Christmas where he becomes a tramp roaming the English countryside, going native in his own country.

1932   Writes "A Scullion's Diary," which is rejected by, among others, T. S. Eliot. Seeks a job that would give him time for writing; becomes a teacher in a private school, despite regarding the job as a dirty swindle.

1933   *Down and Out in Paris and London* published under the pseudonym "George Orwell" by Victor Gollancz; an account of and a meditation upon his experiences as dishwasher and tramp in his tour of the underworld. Good reviews but disappointing sales.

1934   *Burmese Days* is the first of his novels published, by Harper Bros. of New York and later by Gollancz in 1935. Goes to work in a bookshop in Hampstead, London. The beginnings of the "political" Orwell; contacts with certain left-wing people, especially from the Independent Labour party (ILP).

1935   *A Clergyman's Daughter* published: he describes it a good idea but botched by him. Meets Eileen Maud O'Shaughnessy, who earns honours degree in English from Oxford, runs typing agency, then sells it to study psychology at University College, London.

1936   January, Gollancz commissions Orwell to write a book about the condition of the unemployed in the depressed industrial north of England, which is decisive in tilting Orwell into becoming a political writer. Spends two months in Wigan,

Barnsley, and Sheffield, living with ordinary people and deliberately not staying in hotels. *Keep the Aspidistra Flying* published. It reflects his own earlier literary struggles and his current love affair and hopes of marriage. First appearance in his work of theme of apocalyptic destruction: bombing planes, coming war.

9 June, marries Eileen O'Shaughnessy in a church ceremony.

July, outbreak of Spanish Civil War; Franco rebels against the Republican government.

December, leaves London for Spain, visiting Henry Miller in Paris en route. In Barcelona joins POUM (Partido Obrero de Unificacion Marxista), an independent, non-Stalinist, Marxist group with its own separate militia. His aim is to defeat Franco, not to write a book.

1937   March, *The Road to Wigan Pier* published. Gollancz, unhappy about the criticisms of socialism, issues a disclaimer concerning the second, "anti-Marxist" part of the book but tries to blunt the attack by depicting Orwell as a devil's advocate against Socialism.

May, the Communists (Stalinists), attack, imprison, and kill their anarchist (POUM) enemies in Barcelona: a war within a war. A week later Orwell is shot through the neck by a Fascist sniper; on his release from hospital he must go on the run to avoid capture by the Communists. He and Eileen escape into France and return to England in July 1937.

1938   March, tubercular hemorrhage in lung; is hospitalized for six months.

April, *Homage to Catalonia* published by Secker and Warburg (Gollancz had refused because of the book's anti-Communist stance), marking Orwell's decisive break with Stalinism. Begins to acquire his reputation as the moral conscience of the Left. His position is ILP and pacifist. He opposes the approaching war between Great Britain and Germany as an imperialist struggle of no concern to working-class people, simply one band of robbers ranged against another.

September, convalescent trip to Morocco with Eileen.

1939   March, returns to England at same time as the Spanish Republic surrenders to Franco. Meanwhile Chamberlain has capitulated to Hitler at Munich and the Germans occupy Czechoslovakia.

June, *Coming Up for Air* published by Gollancz (still happy to take Orwell's fiction but not his documentary work). Father dies. Still violently antiwar (see his essay, "Not Counting Niggers," an attack upon British imperialism). What changes all this and makes him a patriot (though still a revolutionary) is the astonishing Hitler-Stalin Pact of August 1939. Turns pro-war, recognizing the need to defend the bad against the worse, and rebukes the neutralist Joyce for failing to see this.

3 September, outbreak of War finds him pledging his loyalty even to the detested Chamberlain government. Resigns from pacifist ILP; attempt to enlist fails because of poor health.

1940	March, *Inside the Whale* published. June, joins the Home Guard: "Arm the People" (Orwell's slogan).
1941	*The Lion and the Unicorn* published; upholds English patriotism plus democratic socialism. August, joins BBC as talks producer and broadcaster to India; colleagues include T. S. Eliot and William Empson. Also reviewing for *Time and Tide*, *Tribune*, the *Observer*, *Partisan Review*, and the *Manchester Evening News*. Publishes "Looking Back on the Spanish War," which deals with the importance and difficulty of telling the truth and the menace of propaganda and is to become a leitmotiv in his writing.
1943	19 March, mother dies. Resigns from the BBC, regarding the work as futile. November, becomes literary editor of *Tribune* and "the Socratic gadfly" of the Labour movement.
1944	*Animal Farm* completed in February: no publisher will accept it because of the British alliance with Stalin (T. S. Eliot rejects it for Faber and Faber). June, adopts baby boy, Richard. October, publishes "Raffles and Miss Blandish," linking pornography and power worship and showing the intellectuals as especially vulnerable to the latter.
1945	March, resigns from *Tribune* to become war correspondent for the *Observer* in Paris and Cologne. Meets Hemingway (another war correspondent) in Paris. Eileen dies in Newcastle under anesthetic for a hysterectomy. Orwell returns to Europe after the funeral. August, *Animal Farm* published by Secker and Warburg, an event later signalized by Fred Warburg as his making as a publisher. A great success; Orwell becomes famous overnight. Beginning of the "reviewers' war" about Orwell's attitude to socialism and revolution.
1946	February, publishes *Critical Essays* (published in April in New York as *Dickens, Dali and Others*). Leaves London for the

island of Jura in the Inner Hebrides with his son and a nurse to live at Barnhill, an abandoned farmhouse. Starts to work on *Nineteen Eighty-Four.* Increasingly ill.

1947   December, enters Hairmyres Hospital, East Kilbride, near Glasgow, where he remains for seven months.

1948   July, returns to Jura. Has great difficulty in getting a typist and so types the book himself, greatly injuring his health.

1949   January, enters sanatorium in Cranham, Gloucestershire. Negotiations for publishing *Nineteen Eighty-Four.* The Book-of-the-Month Club in the United States wants the book without the Newspeak appendix and Goldstein's essay—Orwell refuses despite knowing this was worth at least £40,000. Book-of-the-Month relents and takes the whole book.

8 June, *Nineteen Eighty-Four* published by Secker and Warburg, in New York by Harcourt Brace on 13 June. Instantaneous and outstanding success.

September, admitted to University College Hospital, London. Ironic that he should be a dying man when he achieves fame and success—although there is doubt as to how well he knew his own condition.

13 October, marries Sonia Brownell. Plans to go to Switzerland on discharge from hospital.

1950   21 January, final hemorrhage, dies at once and alone. Following his instructions is buried, not cremated, according to the rites of the Church of England at the Church of All Saints, Sutton Courtenay, Oxfordshire.

1

HISTORICAL CONTEXT

Regrettably, one must still begin by insisting that *Nineteen Eighty-Four* is a work of literature and not of politics. Too many readers still come to it determined to use it as propaganda for one side or the other, as cold war warrior or bulwark of socialism. Yet as a novel it resists absorption into the propaganda machine of any state or sect. It is a fiction, and we must resist the temptation to treat it as a model of the real world or as echo chamber for our own political predilections. Above all, we must not coerce it into saying what we wish to hear any more than we would *Tom Jones* or *Vanity Fair*. Like them, it is to be judged by literary, not political, criteria.

This is, admittedly, difficult in view of Orwell's own assertion made in 1946 that his chief aim for the previous ten years had been "to make political writing into an art."[1] For Orwell understanding the world is simply the prelude to changing it; he is a didactic writer, a man with a mission, the antipodal opposite of the detached aesthete immured in his ivory tower, caring only for the creation of beauty and heedless of the sufferings of humanity. He will sacrifice art itself when life is in the other scale; witness his conscious violation of the artistic integrity of *Homage to Catalonia* by interpolating a chunk of newspaper quotations in order to repudiate the vilification of his friends in Barcelona.[2] Some readers complain that *Nineteen Eighty-Four* is similarly spoiled by thrusting into the middle of the action long chapters from Goldstein's book and by tacking on the Appendix on Newspeak at the close of the story. It may be that "pure" literature cannot digest such gobbets and should not be asked to do so. Orwell, however, is no purist in the tradition of Flaubert, Proust, and Joyce but a man trying to save us from the wrath to come, and he needs Goldstein's book and the Appendix to alert us to the danger. How badly is proved by his readiness to sacrifice around £40,000 when he refused the Book-of-the-Month Club offer to take the book on condition he leave these sections out.[3] What I have written I have written: Pilate's uncompromising answer is echoed in Orwell's heroic obduracy, and neither the cavils of aesthetes nor the temptations of affluence can make him yield. A fidelity to politics compels him to write his book as he does.

Nevertheless, Orwell's declared aim was to transform politics into art, and when he decided to write a novel and not a tract, he was paying homage to the primacy of the creative imagination. It follows that the meaning of the political concepts within *Nineteen Eighty-Four* is defined by the context of the fiction as a whole and not by the external world. The purpose of this study is to present Orwell as a great, underrated creative writer who has not yet received just recognition for what he achieved in *Nineteen Eighty-Four*.

There are hints of *The Waste Land* in *Nineteen Eighty-Four*, but it is Eliot the critic who can help us to establish a framework for understanding the novel.[4] In "Tradition and the Individual Talent," Eliot insists that no artist has his complete meaning alone: "You cannot value him alone; you must set him, for contrast and comparison, among the dead."[5] Eliot's basic metaphor is not that fluid, ever-changing stream of history that so terrifies Winston Smith[6] but a kind of artistic Stonehenge, with the existing monuments forming an ideal order among themselves, fixed, powerful, immovable—but not unchangeable. This order can be and is modified by the introduction of the new work of art among them. The new work of art takes its place in the existing order and, in doing so, alters it, however slightly. The relations, proportions, and values of each work of art toward the whole are readjusted, and this is conformity between the old and the new. The past is altered by the present as much as the present is directed by the past. When a new work of art is created, something simultaneously happens to all the works of art that precede it.

What could be more pertinent to *Nineteen Eighty-Four* than this discussion of the relationship between past and present? It is what the book is really about. When O'Brien asks if they should toast the future, Winston replies, "To the past" (p. 143), and O'Brien gravely agrees that the past is more important. Later O'Brien openly declares his venomous antagonism to the past: "Above all we do not allow the dead to rise up against us" (p. 202). It is just as appropriate that the still-undefeated Winston should wake up with the name Shakespeare on his lips.

Orwell's book upholds the importance of the past, of tradition, not only by what it says but by what it is—by being the kind of work that Eliot describes as taking its place in the existing monumental order. The proof of its creativity can be seen in the way it urges us to look again, "for contrast and comparison," at certain great writers and works of the past, most notably *Gulliver's Travels* and *Paradise Lost*, but also at Fielding, Dickens, Dostoyevsky, H. G. Wells, Jack London, Gissing, Aldous Huxley, Arthur Koestler, T. S. Eliot himself, as well as that basic myth of Western man, Jack the Giant-Killer. This study will attempt to demonstrate this creativity, especially in relation to Winston's Gulliverian journey in Oceania, to the sinful lovers and the angry God so evocative of Milton, and to the shocking fate of the would-be giant-killer in modern times. Here, rather than in politics or sociology, is the clue to the meaning of *Nineteen Eighty-Four*. Moreover, Eliot's principle of reciprocity holds true, for our rereading of Swift and Milton is influenced by Orwell's novel just as surely as it was shaped by them. We must, above all, situate *Nineteen Eighty-Four* in literature.

The art, nevertheless, was fed by a specific historical milieu, and the novel comes as the logical development, if not culmination, of Orwell's sociopolitical concerns. By the early 1930s he was beginning to attract attention as a writer at a time when there was a growing literary interest in working-class life. It was a period of industrial depression and massive unemployment, worsened in Great Britain by abysmal standards of housing, health, and nutrition and by an entrenched class system. Many, seeking an answer to these problems in left-wing politics, hailed the new Soviet experiment as the wave of the future. At the same time, however, the rise of fascism and, more decisively, of nazism on the Continent heralded the specter of European war. In 1936 General Franco led a right-wing rebellion against the Republican government of Spain in what proved to be a rehearsal for the greater conflict that erupted three years later.[7]

Orwell was intimately involved with these upheavals, supporting socialism against capitalism and Stalinism alike, living for a time among the industrial unemployed in the north of England (see *The Road to Wigan Pier*), volunteering to fight for Republican Spain (see *Homage to Catalonia*). Since his return to England from Burma, he had been obsessed with the condition of those at the base of the social pyramid—dropouts, tramps, outcasts—believed that to tell their story he had to join them. Most of the people he wrote about, real and fictional, fit into the category of outcast, and, in sharing their experiences, he himself became misfit, rebel, class renegade. In his earlier fiction of the 1930s (*Burmese Days, A Clergyman's Daughter, Keep the Aspidistra Flying, Coming Up for Air*) his protagonists attempt, with varying degrees of failure, to rebel against their environment and conditioning. *Animal Farm* similarly tells the Aesopian story of an abortive attempt by animals to end their exploitation by people and build a just society, but they succeed only in installing the pigs as their new masters in a regime as harshly oppressive as the old. Many saw in this fable an explicit disillusionment with the Bolshevik Revolution; some, going further, detected a critique of revolution itself.

Orwell disliked and distrusted both Churchill and Stalin, capitalism and communism, and in the Tehran and Yalta conferences, where the clearly victorious allies planned the division of Europe after Hitler's downfall, he saw only a cynical plan for perpetuating an unjust system in which some privileged animals would continue to be more equal than others. Here is the germ of the political situation in *Nine-*

teen Eighty-Four: a world divided and ruled by three superpowers, the inheritors of the United States, the Soviet Union, and China, ostensibly enemies, yet in reality, as the "War is Peace" section of Goldstein's book shows, covertly maintaining each other forever. What *Nineteen Eighty-Four* does is to gather almost all the ideas, arguments, and problems of Orwell's previous work, fiction and nonfiction alike, and concentrate them in their most frightening, challenging form.[8] To make the continuity even more striking, it does so by using an infrastructure, immediately recognizable from his other fiction, in which the isolated hero-victim tries vainly to resist a hostile society and to seek a better life but is forced, after a series of misunderstandings and disappointments, to capitulate.[9] Once again Orwell's own previous fiction, rather than a political treatise like James Burnham's *The Managerial Revolution,* is the better guide to the meaning of his last book. But with one crucial, catastrophically shocking difference, which I shall later examine in detail. Never before, in the most sordid incident, abject character, or depressing circumstance, had Orwell depicted so humiliating a defeat as the fall of Winston Smith or shown the human spirit so irrievably shattered. To explain why he now chose to do so is the purpose of this book.

2

THE IMPORTANCE OF
THE WORK

In an age enthralled by ideology, when truth has been brutally frog-marched to suit the requirements of various political orthodoxies, left and right, and when many intellectuals, betraying their vocation, have been too depressingly willing to prostitute their gifts to the service of power and expediency, it is at once an inspiration and a boon to encounter a writer like Orwell and a work like *Nineteen Eighty-Four*.[1] Orwell is that marvel—a propagandist who repudiates lies, a man whose dedication to a cause excludes consent to perjury; even the Just Society comes too dear when the cost is the integrity of the self. He is the prime example in our time of the writer as hero, refusing to divorce politics from ethics, insisting on the unwelcome, unfashionable truth, the inconvenient truth that the *apparatchik* is so ready to suppress when it is a scandal to the faithful. Orwell is not afraid of scandal; he boldly enters Ephesus to denounce Diana. It is this moral greatness, this gift for unpalatable truth, that is the key to his continuing relevance, making him a living presence, a contemporary writer almost forty years after his death, someone who must be read, especially by his opponents. His official biographer rightly describes him as a political thinker of genuine stature and a supreme political writer, the finest in English since Jonathan Swift, and asserts that *Nineteen Eighty-Four* stands toward the twentieth as Hobbes's masterpiece, *Leviathan*, does toward the seventeenth century.[2] These are high claims. The aim of this study is to vindicate them, to present them, startling as they are, as the truth.

But who are Orwell's opponents, those most bound, for their own sakes and in their own interests, to submit themselves to this book? There is no more important question concerning *Nineteen Eighty-Four* than identifying the object of its attack. From the moment of publication, there have been too many readers, especially on the Right, who assume their own immunity; someone else is being attacked, their own enemies naturally, and they embrace Orwell as a political ally, of their party even if he did not yet know it and did not live to discover it.[3] They observe, rightly, that *Animal Farm* is an attack on Stalinism and conveniently ignore that it just as devastatingly indicts General Motors; at the fable's end Napoleon and Pilkington are indistinguishable. The neoconservative ideologues continue to hijack *Animal Farm*, but it remains an act of piracy, for only by violence can the book be made to travel in their direction.

There has been a similar seizure of *Nineteen Eighty-Four*, leading to a similar distortion of destination. It is not, neoconservative persuasions notwithstanding, simply an attack on Stalinism or socialism or the centralized state but a composite nightmare, fusing the worst elements of our world, East and West, Left and Right, in one hideous scenario, one monstrous collage, of a possible fate. That Orwell abhorred the Soviet system no one will deny, and in this sense his book is the final blow in a campaign waged since his Spanish experience. But it is just as undeniable that Orwell did not look eastward for the names of his dystopia, Oceania and Airstrip One, or for its currency, the dollar, and the porn and prole-feed manufactured by Big Brother have indisputably found a cosier home in the capitalist West than behind the iron curtain. The greatness of *Nineteen Eighty-Four* is that it transcends the purely historical conditions that produced it; its argument does not depend on one specific application, one single historical instance, one simple set of correspondences. It is a matter of

permanent truth rather than of transient political excitement. If Stalinism were ever to be relegated to a historical footnote, *Nineteen
Eighty-Four* would still retain its validity as a horrendous warning
against a possible catastrophe.

The neoconservatives who claim Orwell as an ally are as mistaken
as the zealots of the Left who denounce him as a renegade. No one is
Orwell's ally in *Nineteen Eighty-Four,* for he deliberately chooses not
to have any. In this text we are all Orwell's opponents. He comes, like
his master, Swift, before him, not to condemn some and favor others
but to summon all to repentance before it is too late. He had once,
only half-facetiously, compared himself to one of the comminatory
Old Testament prophets, but the flippant, self-derisory tone should
not blind us to the anguish suffered or the animus vented (*CEJL,*
1:164).[4] The joke of Orwell as frustrated prophet sent to recall a back-
sliding people to ancient verities is no laughing matter. The greatness
of *Nineteen Eighty-Four* will be properly registered only by those who
sense the personal nature of the indictment and do not resent it as an
impertinence. *De te fabula* ("thou art the man"): Orwell makes it
plain to the honest reader that it is his story he is telling, not some
pharisaical fulmination against the sins of other men—Stalinists, so-
cialists, or whatever.[5]

Orwell earns the right to be hard on us by being simultaneously
hard on himself. No orthodoxy, his own included, is exempt from the
harshness of his scrutiny. Orwell's celebrated uncompromising honesty
subjects every belief, his most cherished tenets included, to the most
testing reappraisal. His last great book interrogates a mystery: why
has the socialism he believes in so heartrendingly failed? Deeper than
this, subtending all politics, is the problematic nature of the human
being, the ultimate human mystery. Orwell's relentless inquiry into the
political iniquities of our time led him inevitably to analyze the animal
that committed them, and, if he is to the twentieth what Hobbes was
to the seventeenth century, it is because for him, too, the political analysis is finally grounded on certain human revelations. It is at once a
measure of his honesty and a proof of his relevance that his discoveries
should even yet be so difficult to accept.

No one suffered more from these discoveries than Orwell himself. As humanist he regards life as noble and people as dignified; as socialist he believes that a rational, Marxist reconstruction of society is the one solution to economic chaos; as atheist he neither believes in nor needs a God. These are his sanctities, the hallowed pieties by which he lived. In *Nineteen Eighty-Four* we watch Orwell nerving himself to question all three. And so three dreadful possibilities ambush us: what if life is incurably vile, socialism an impossible dream, atheistic people insufficient to the imposed task? The book is itself a kind of communal Room 101 in which our worst fears take shape and move among us. How stunningly successful the book is in embodying these fears is attested by the tributes it has deservedly evoked. One critic calls it the best antidote to the totalitarian disease so far produced;[6] another declares that it has "become part of the common imaginative heritage of the Western world," so that the very date is now inextricably linked with the concept of oppressive government.[7] Another asserts that "no political book, whether fiction or nonfiction . . . has passed more thoroughly into the English language and the popular consciousness of the Western world than Orwell's dark masterpiece."[8] The book has supplied a whole new set of words—*Big Brother, doublethink, ownlife, Newspeak, Thought Police*—to political discourse: Orwell, whose creative power is often underrated, has received the supreme accolade of the great creative writer: even those who have not read his book recognize its terminology.

Nevertheless the central argument of this study is that *Nineteen Eighty-Four* has not been treated with the full seriousness it deserves. Orwell's premonitions of disaster are not to be accounted for simply in terms of politico-economic foul-ups. He himself despised and feared those who sought to explain the human predicament as a species of mechanical breakdown, errors of the surface, malfunctions in the social machine that the engineers could be left to correct (*CEJL*, 1:583, 2:304–5, 3:126, 4:541). He dreaded, rightly or wrongly, a deformation of human nature and traced it, astonishingly in view of his own atheism, to the fallout from the religious fission of the modern age (*CEJL*, 3:123).[9] For almost two centuries social critics had warned that bourgeois society was living off the accumulated moral capital of traditional religion and traditional moral philosophy and that once this capital was depleted, bourgeois society would find its legitimacy ever more questionable. Orwell is the moral accountant who, having taken it upon himself to examine the books, brings the dire news of ethical bankruptcy.

In doing so he offends those who still believe that bourgeois, liberal society can satisfactorily survive on its own rational resources, its own utilitarian axioms, without any need of a faith that exalts love and community above egoism and self-interest. It is the ideological presuppositions of modernity itself that Orwell reveals as bankrupt. At the same time he affronts the radicals by declaring that their cure for these evils is even worse than the disease itself, since they are inevitably, if heedlessly, conducting us to a kingdom of terror where Big Brother rather than the forgotten father of traditional religion is the savage God to whom all must submit. Liberals and radicals alike will not find their favorite predilections being flattered in Orwell, but those who prefer truth to flattery will not be deterred on that account. Flattery, says Burke, corrupts both the receiver and the giver; to read Orwell as he deserves is to preserve oneself from at least this particular corruption.[10]

3

CRITICAL RECEPTION

From the outset two facts are incontestable about *Nineteen Eighty-Four*: it was hugely successful and highly contentious. A first edition of 25,000 copies was published on 8 June 1949. Within a year nearly 50,000 copies had been sold in Great Britain, and 170,000 copies had been sold in the United States, 190,000 in the Book-of-the-Month Club edition. It was condensed in the *Reader's Digest* and has been translated into more than twenty languages. It has never stopped selling and has achieved the status of a modern classic.

What is the precise nature of the book that millions of people have been reading? Some early critics found in it a satire of the contemporary social and political scene. Veronica Wedgwood and Julian Symons, rejecting the idea of a dystopian fantasy in the tradition of *Brave New World*, traced the extension of certain discernible tendencies of 1948 extrapolated into the "near future" of 1984 by a simple reversal of digits—the austerity and rationing of postwar Britain were intensified in the chronic shortages of Oceania.[1] V. S. Pritchett described it as a "satirical pamphlet," Swiftian in provenance and savagery, a corrosive satire on the moral corruption of absolute power.[2] Despite the futuristic setting, all three agreed that the book is a satire of Orwell's own immediate milieu.

Other critics, especially among the first wave of reviewers in the United States, hailed it as an attack on a specific political system: Stalinist communism. Some saw it as a comprehensive antisocialist polemic, with Ingsoc standing for the British Labour party. Oceania was interpreted as the prophecy of a penitent leftist who had recanted and was telling us what would and must happen if the free enterprise system were not resolutely defended. These right-wing apologists were paradoxically reinforced by certain Communist critics, seething at what they considered the scurrilous attack of a renegade writer on the Soviet Union.[3]

But from the beginning eminent voices challenged this interpretation. The historian Golo Mann, son of the great German novelist, was among the first to argue that the book was warning rather than prophecy and that nazism as well as communism had provided the material for denunciation. Mann deplored the fact that some Americans had already turned *Animal Farm* into crude anti-Soviet propaganda and clearly feared a similar fate for the new novel.[4] Lionel Trilling also insisted that the book was not a specific attack on communism or socialism but a general indictment of all those forces in society that make for dehumanization.[5] Orwell had produced an imaginative treatise on totalitarianism, cutting across all ideologies, warning of the threat to humanity should any government, of whatever political complexion, assume absolute power.

Those advocating this view had the great advantage of being able to cite Orwell himself as witness. Distressed by what he took to be either the misunderstanding or, worse, the deliberate distortion of his text by the enemies of socialism, Orwell dictated his own explication to be issued by his publisher, Fred Warburg, as a press release. Oceania was not what would but what could happen if intellectuals of all colors continued to be contaminated by a totalitarian outlook. The road to Miniluv is the direction in which our world is traveling, but it is not an inevitable terminus. The book is located in a Britain of the future in order to expose the complacent English belief that they are an immaculate conception, pharisaically exempt from the sins of other men: "to emphasise that the English-speaking races are not innately better than anyone else and that totalitarianism, if not fought against, could triumph anywhere" (*CEJL*, 4:564). Evil empires may emerge as easily in the West as in the East; totalitarian ideas have taken root in the minds of intellectuals everywhere (*CEJL*, 4:564). For Orwell intellectuals as a class, not some subset restricted by geographical or ideological criteria, are guilty. The malaise is not confined to the East or to the Left. The most serious single error in reading Orwell's book is the delusion that someone else is under attack. But Orwell is just as anxious to scotch the fallacy of inevitability as he is to advance the axiom of ubiquitous guilt. None of this need happen if people are brave and decent enough. Hence the moral is: don't let it happen—it depends on you.

Despite his willingness to issue this press release, Warburg had supplied a very different summary after his first reading of the typescript in December 1948 when instructing his firm to ensure the book's early publication. Then he had drawn parallels with Swift and Dostoyevsky in assessing Orwell's terrifying text. He predicted that it would be a vote winner for Winston Churchill and the Conservative party, revealing, so he judged, "a final breach between Orwell and Socialism, not the socialism of equality and human brotherhood which clearly Orwell no longer expects from socialist parties, but the socialism of marxism and the managerial revolution."[6] The book is bleak and despairing, denying readers any scintilla of hope: "here is a study in pessimism unrelieved, except perhaps by the thought that, if a man can conceive *1984,* he can also will to avoid it." Far from censuring such despair, Warburg identifies it as the source of the book's undoubted greatness, and he refers to "the giant movement of thought which Orwell has set in motion in *1984.*" Yet for Warburg, as for Dr. Johnson with *King Lear,* the greatness is inseparable from the anguish evoked, and he praises *Nineteen Eighty-Four* in the same accent of fascinated abhorrence wrested from Johnson by Shakespeare's masterpiece: "It is a great book, but I pray I may be spared from reading another like it for years to come."[7] Whatever our final conclusion, there is something valid in this reaction to the text, and it is surely preferable to the smugness of those critics who revisit Oceania all too readily and gleefully in a one-eyed search for ammunition against their enemies.

Remarkably these initial contrasting reactions served to establish the boundaries of the different critical divisions persisting since 1949 to our own day, so that it is possible to trace the developments and continuities of existing opinions to their first ancestry and original expression. The critical battle to appropriate *Nineteen Eighty-Four* that erupted on publication is still being waged today, with substantially the same standpoints being defended, the same strategies pursued, only with more sophisticated critical weaponries. There is, in fact, a striking parallel with that inconclusive, never-ending war in *Nineteen Eighty-Four* among the three superpowers for possession of the disputed quadrilateral of territory lying between their inviolable realms. Orwell's book has similarly become the arena of a power struggle as contending groups battle to annex it for their own cause.

"Dickens is one of those writers who are well worth stealing" (*CEJL*, 1:454): Orwell, unconsciously foretelling his own fate, began his essay on the great Victorian, pointing out that Marxists, Catholics, and liberals have all paid him the compliment of claiming him as their own. The bodysnatchers have paid *Nineteen Eighty-Four* the same high tribute, and, just as with Dickens, the rivalry reflects the importance of the text. If people contend only for what they judge to be valuable, then *Nineteen Eighty-Four* must be one of the most treasured properties of our age.

There are three main ways of responding to the text. There is, first, the insistence that the book is, above all, a satire, an essentially comic warning concerning a possible but not inevitable fate. This view allows one to continue regarding Orwell as a loyal socialist who never had any serious doubts as to the eventual predetermined victory of the common people. The book's prime conditional must be translated into an imperious indicative: there is hope, and it is in the proles. And not just hope but an assurance akin to the believer's when he declares: "I know that my Redeemer liveth." Orwell knows that the redeemer has appeared in Oceania. The common people must and will arise one day and destroy Big Brother, a triumph as certain as God's over Satan in

Paradise Lost or Sarastro's over the Queen of Night in *The Magic Flute*. Yet O'Brien says otherwise and finally converts Winston to his view: the proles are futile creatures who can be left "free," since nothing they do or can conceivably do will ever threaten Big Brother. There is no hope in the proles.

This belief, however, simply exposes O'Brien and Winston as the chief targets of the satire. The book was written to lambast the folly of the power worshipper. O'Brien's paean to power identifies him as Orwell's butt, a fool unable to see that in the long run his horrendous system cannot endure. The mysticism of cruelty, for which Orwell has been condemned, is present in the text, but O'Brien, not Orwell, is its purveyor and its dupe. Precisely this blunder makes him the text's gull, and Winston errs in becoming his foolish follower—hence the comedy of the final view of the alcoholic wreck, gin-stained tears trickling down his nose, recalling the old drunken prole whom he met as a child during the bombing raid, gazing in fatuous adoration at the face of his beloved violator (p. 29). What an idiot: this, or something akin, should be our reaction. Those who are tender hearted by nature may be permitted a twinge of pity, to feel compassion for the fool come to so sorry a destination. Life, we are told, is a tragedy for those who feel, a comedy for those who think.[8] Satire demands thinkers. If we read this satire with the detachment required, we shall appreciate the humor, admittedly harsh, perhaps even black, of the situation. The book is comédie noire, gallows humor, a black joke. Seen from this perspective, Winston is an object of derision rather than pity.[9]

The "feelers" may sympathize with a sap; the thinkers will laugh at a failure. The one option forbidden us by the text is to identify with Winston. Here is no image of our future fate, no distressing complicity or embarrassing relationship, but a cautionary, comic tale, a satiric exposé of certain blunders plus a confident exhortation not to repeat them. We need not, must not, be Winston, and the text, properly read, will teach us how to avoid it. There is no cause for fear, far less for panic or despair. All we need do is keep our nerve and sense of humor, laugh at O'Brien's wild claims, and maintain our faith in the ultimate invincibility of ordinary folk. The proles are immortal and insuperable; O'Brien, Winston, and the other power worshippers are losers at last.

There is strong external evidence to support this view. Never once did Orwell renounce his faith in socialism, however much he attacked its contemporary distortions. Even his shocking experience in Spain left him more assuredly socialist than ever: "I have seen wonderful things and at last really believe in Socialism which I never did before" (*CEJL*, 1:301). His rebuff to the Duchess of Atholl's invitation in 1945 to join her League for European Freedom makes his position indisputably clear: "I cannot associate myself with an essentially Conservative body which claims to defend democracy in Europe, but has nothing to say about British Imperialism. . . . I belong to the Left and must work within it, much as I hate Russian totalitarianism and its poisonous influence in this country" (*CEJL*, 3:370, 4:49). There is, in addition, his concern at his book's perversion into an antisocialist tract and his resolve to put a stop to this by explaining his own intentions in *Nineteen Eighty-Four*.

Yet this very appeal by critics to external evidence betrays an uneasiness. The enlistment of the biography to elucidate the text, the life to define the art, proves that the book is not so manifestly clear as some critics apparently wish. Why invoke external evidence at all if the internal evidence, the text itself, already supports the desired interpretation? The biographical approach to critical judgment is often irrelevant and sometimes misleading. To denounce *Nineteen Eighty-Four* as the pessimistic howl of a dying man, for example, is as impermissible as defending the book by pointing to the nobility of its author's life; the text itself is what should concern us. Bernard Crick, the most prominent of those urging the comic satire view, perhaps falters in this concern when he scolds Orwell for not making his meaning sufficiently clear.[10] True, he also chides those who find the text despairing for their inability to read satire, but Orwell shares the blame for not making it plain that his book envisages the triumph of the common people and the victory of socialism. Crick explains Orwell's carelessness in leaving his text so vulnerable to misinterpretation. Orwell had long since grown used to writing for a relatively small readership who knew him and his politics and who could accordingly be trusted to interpret his work correctly. When the great success of *Animal Farm* and *Nineteen Eighty-Four* made him a world author, this cosy affinity between writer and public ceased, but Orwell continued to write in his old, incautious style. The consequences have been disastrous. People who know little or nothing about him misread his last two books, indifferent to or ignorant of his intentions in writing them. Sturdy socialist commonsense is misconstrued as surrender to despair. Orwell is culpable, and this is why *Nineteen Eighty-Four* is "a flawed masterpiece both of literature and of political thought. We need to know why hope lies in the Proles."[11] But *do* we, even if Orwell, for his own strategic purposes, perhaps meant to deny this hope? It is, after all, his book, and we are many years too late to persuade him to write it differently.

A howl of despair, a failure of nerve, a surrender to irrational fears, an act of betrayal, deliberate or inadvertent, are precisely what some disapproving critics detect in the book. Attention need not be paid to the extreme Communist slanders of a renegade who, for love of money, went rushing to the capitalist publishers with a couple of horror comics maligning the Revolution.[12] The notion of Orwell as literary prostitute is even more blunder than slander, for, in so egregiously putting cart before horse, it exhibits an inexcusable historical ignorance. The world, not Orwell, turned its coat, and he suddenly became famous for saying what he had long and unpopularly said. *Animal Farm* failed to find a publisher in the capitalist West because it attacked Stalin.

The strictures of critics such as Isaac Deutscher and Raymond Williams are a very different matter; these eminent men of the Left find something radically unsound in Orwell's book. Deutscher's notorious attack on Orwell for his alleged surrender to the mysticism of cruelty will continue to command support from some readers disturbed at the irrational thesis of power for power's sake and of a society committed to the boot in the face forever; while those who believe that, precisely here, Orwell has unearthed the appalling, manic truth of totalitarianism, will, even in disagreeing with it, welcome

Deutscher's essay as a necessary negative contribution toward our full awareness of this revelation.[13] Williams similarly reproached Orwell for his "totalitarian way of warning against totalitarianism," his abandonment of cool, discriminating judgment to go whoring after "the irrational projection inspiring either terror or hate."[14] Orwell, however inadvertently, has sold the pass to the totalitarian foe: "The warning that the world could be going that way became, in the very absoluteness of the fiction, an imaginative submission to its inevitability."[15] There will always be readers who find *Nineteen Eighty-Four* more conspicuous for its dark despair than for its cleansing comedy.

The third main group are the neoconservative critics who, because of the political nature of Orwell's book and its continuous enormous success, have sought to claim it as a manifesto of their own views and to annex Orwell as an ideological blood brother. Prominent among these are the American critics Russell Kirk and Norman Podhoretz. For Kirk, Orwell was a leftist by accident whose socialism was essentially a sentimental reaction to the conditions of life. His pessimism finally deepened into misanthropy, and, bereft of any consoling religious belief, he fell into despair: "When a man like Orwell begins to see what State Socialism really must become in the age that is dawning, he writes *1984*, grits his teeth, and dies."[16] Podhoretz speculates that if Orwell had lived into the 1980s, his political views would have shifted from socialism to neoconservatism and frankly explains why he wants Orwell so badly: "It is, after all, no small thing to have the greatest political writer of the age on one's side: it gives confidence, authority, and weight to one's own political views."[17] No doubt, but to take what is not yours is still regarded as theft. Is it any wonder, Podhoretz asks, that the neoconservatives claim Orwell as a guiding spirit when his excoriation of the unpatriotic, deraciné English intelligentsia is echoed in their own attack upon American left-wing intellectuals today?[18] Other critics, however, respond either by accusing Podhoretz of partisan, judiciously edited quotations taken out of context in order to push a dead man into a camp he detested or by dismissing all such speculation about a living Orwell's present political orientation as foolish.[19] Privacy is certainly a major theme—and a major deprivation—in *Nineteen Eighty-Four,* but Orwell's attack is surely on totalitarianism rather than socialism. Neoconservatives may argue that, finally, privacy and individual freedom are inextricably linked to a free market economy, that only a total repudiation of socialism, planning, and the centralized state can guarantee the private lives that Winston and Julia vainly crave; but even were all this true, it would not prove that Orwell agreed. Neoconservatives may assume that socialism and totalitarianism are identical or that the former is merely a posting stage on the road to the latter but should not assume that Orwell concurs.

There are other major areas of dispute concerning the book, one of these being the extent to which it may be accepted as in some sense Orwell's last testament. It was written while he was dying, and some argue that its alleged pessimism is directly related to Orwell's fatal illness, a position partially supported by his own remark that the book would not have been so gloomy if he had not been so ill (*CEJL,* 4:507, 513, 536). Other critics will not allow it to be read as Orwell's intentional dying word; it just happened to be the last book he wrote before he happened to die.[20] One danger of this despair-of-a-dying-man view is that it can be employed to dodge the accusation by belittling the achievement, implying that the book is as it is because of the author's sickness. The text has more to do with the sad condition of Orwell's lungs than with the world either as it is or might be; we are looking at Orwell's physiological doom rather than our own possible destiny. It is apparently a comfort to some people to neuter the insights of the artist by explaining them in terms of disease or insanity. Swift's "Voyage to the Houyhnhnms" is less disturbing as the work of a madman, and *Nineteen Eighty-Four* becomes safer when traced to the despair of a terminal illness. Yet the power of these works is commensurate with their ability to hurt, and we cheat ourselves and diminish them when we practice these reductive stratagems upon them.

The same is true of those Freudian theories that seek to explain the novel in terms of some psychological wound allegedly suffered by Orwell in childhood, especially at the prep school he so disliked. Anthony West advances this theory of Orwell's paranoiac art, but to try to reduce Orwell's achievement to these neuroses is as misleading as it is naive.[21] The argument that Oceania is merely a monstrous magnification of the school that he denounced in "Such, Such Were the Joys" is a sad devaluation of Orwell's book, as well as a flagrant example of the genetic fallacy—the assumption that we have solved a work when we disclose its origins. Murray Sperber nails the fallacy when he comments that "his plan is much grander than an attack on his old school. Orwell transforms his experiences . . . into a world of fears and fantasies that will encompass all people, during all periods of their lives, for all of history."[22] *Nineteen Eighty-Four* is a great book precisely because it is not a personal neurosis or a private nightmare but a terrifying evocation of our collective fears, our cultural delirium. It is the age that is sick, not its diagnostician.

Any responsible reading of the book must do justice to all the evidence, external and internal, to author and to book alike, to the man who lives and to the mind that creates, to the heroism of the life and to the inescapable textual despair. This despair is surely inseparable from the celebrated honesty, the resolve to prove every belief, however cherished, in the crucible of experience. Yet to use a word like *despair* about Orwell is both hazardous and potentially misleading. One immediately feels compelled to add a qualifying adjective such as *calculated* or *provisional* or *strategic*. Reading Orwell makes exceptional demands on our power to discriminate, to follow him in his sometimes startling changes of direction, confident that what initially seems contradiction or inconsistency is really testimony to the profound rightness of the man, the superb dexterity of the moral athlete. Never was the discrimination so necessary or so difficult as in our response to *Nineteen Eighty-Four*. The book is a delicate balance, a tightrope walk between despair and exhortation, where to lean, however slightly, in either direction ensures the critic's fall.

Finally, the chief critical division, subtending all others, is between those who regard Orwell as an optimist and those who regard him as a pessimist. A survey of the critics since 1949 reveals an inveterate tendency to make him too much of the one or too much of the other. Those who find only surrender in the text, author's as well as character's, miss the fact that Orwell is still striving to save us and that this dark book can still be our means of rescue; in Warburg's words, "if a man can conceive *1984*, he can also will to avoid it."[23] The very existence of the book, the fact that it got itself written, is, paradoxically, cause for hope. Would Orwell have labored to write it, killing himself in the process, if he had throught it would do no good and had truly, irremediably despaired?

And yet, further paradox, even to say this, necessary though it be, may so easily promote in us that fatal complacency that *Nineteen Eighty-Four* set out to destroy. We are not to be saved by a deputy but to be our own redeemers: that is Orwell's intention. The book is not to be our salvation but our means to salvation. The use we make of it will be all important. For this reason there is something dismayingly counterproductive in the often ingenious theories of those who point to the book itself, to Orwell's words segregated from any consequence, as proof of an optimistic outcome. We are assured, for example, that the real end of the book is not the debacle of Room 101 or the final spectacle of the abject alcoholic but the Appendix with its encouraging message that Newspeak is still not triumphant and that its complete adoption has been postponed to so distant a date as 2050 (p. 247).[24] The implication is that good literature is stubbornly resistant to tyranny; books themselves, what Milton called the lifeblood of master spirits, inlcuding *Nineteen Eighty-Four*, will frustrate Big Brother: the Word will save us.

The most sophisticated of such theories is that advanced by André Brink when he, too, argues that the pessimistic end of the book is not the end of the story and advocates a deconstruction of the text from the point of view of time and tense.[25] Since the book is written in the past tense, the narrator must be reflecting upon Winston's story from a vantage point even further into the future than 1984. He is looking back at events already concluded, something he could conceivably do only if Big Brother's regime has become extinct in the meantime. The narrator lives, writes, and judges from a framework of values radically different from that of Big Brother. The "today" referred to in the Appendix (p. 241) is neither 1948 when Orwell sat writing in Jura nor

1984 itself but a day long after Winston's defeat. This "today" is not Orwell's or Winston's but the narrator's. It follows that the memory holes and the whole business of reshaping the past cannot have been successful, for how, then, could we know Winston's story at all? Orwell's original title for his novel was *The Last Man in Europe,* and O'Brien taunts Winston by telling him that he is the last man, the last of his kind, that his surrender means the end of the contest (p. 214). The existence of the narrator disproves this, the very fact that we can read Winston's story proves in itself that *Nineteen Eighty-Four* ends not in Big Brother's triumph but in the vindication of the creative act, the written word.

This is a much more original argument than, say, Asimov's simplistic insistence that, since hitherto in history every tyrant has fallen, so we can assume that Big Brother will bite the dust too: "Big Brothers *do* die, or at least they have so far, and when they die, the government changes, always for the milder."[26] This overlooks Orwell's claims concerning the unprecedented nature of modern totalitarianism, his attack on the liberals for assuming that the downfall of the Old Inquisition somehow guarantees that of any future equivalent (*CEJL,* 1:413–14, 2:298, 3:231, 4:465). So deeply did Orwell feel this that he put the same sentiment into the demotic idiom of his hero in *Coming Up for Air*: "Old Hitler's something different. So's Joe Stalin. . . . They're after something quite new . . . something that's never been heard of before."[27] What Nazis and Communists only partly achieved has been brought to perfection, claims O'Brien, by Ingsoc (p. 209). Those who agree with Asimov are treating *Nineteen Eighty-Four* as Winston treats Goldstein's book. The best books, he comforts himself, are those that tell you what you already know (p. 160). We already "know" that freedom is inextinguishable, that the mind is inviolable, that tyranny cannot endure, and all the other truisms of the liberal tradition. But perhaps Orwell has written a different kind of book, one of those select few that tell you what you did not know and, moreover, would prefer to go on not knowing.

Brink, however, does not predict that Big Brother must or will fail. He argues, citing the text itself as evidence, that he has failed. The narrator writes Winston's story at a time when Winston is dead but his values have triumphed. The spirit of man has conquered, as the once-defiant Winston said it would. All's well that ends well. Language itself is on the side of the angels. The past-tense narrative of *Nineteen Eighty-Four* is proof of Big Brother's defeat: the Word is triumphant.

Many will remain unpersuaded, continuing to believe that words without deeds are futile, convinced that Orwell's whole purpose is an incitement toward action; we are to read and act. Nevertheless, the originality and forcefulness of these new critical strategies impel us to add a third incontestable fact about *Nineteen Eighty-Four* to the two with which this chapter opened: after nearly forty years Orwell's book still retains the power to provoke fresh thought and fruitful discussion.

A READING

4

THE INVINCIBLE GIANT

Nineteen Eighty-Four is a modern rendition, chillingly modified, of that basic myth of Western culture, Jack the Giant-Killer. The killing of giants is the metaphor that instinctively presents itself to Western man whenever he feels called upon to define his historical role and mission. Orwell, however, has written a wicked fairy-tale, an antifable, designed, it would seem, not to embolden but to dismay, exalting the giant and emasculating his opponent. Within a few pages we have met the established performers of the familiar tale—hero, giant, princess—each presented in the traditional way. The hero is small and isolated, completely outmatched in physical terms. The giant is huge and omnipresent; the face on the poster is enormous, and the posters, with their penetrating eyes, are everywhere—on every floor within the building, on every commanding corner of the street. The princess is conventionally introduced as distant and unattainable, beautiful but ice cold (the sash around her waist is the sign of this putative frigidity); the hero sees in her someone impossibly beyond his grasp or possession. Frightful giants, beleaguered heroes, wintry maidens: it is always so in the best fairy-tales. In Orwell, too, as in the myth, the woman's role is supporting, subsidiary; the story is about Jack, not Jack and

Jill. Jill is the prize, the reward for the hero's perseverance, and Orwell conforms to the age-old pattern by focusing on the two presiding male personages: the hero and his adversary, Jack and the giant.

These are introduced at once: Winston, smallish, frail, meager, and the ogre, presented mediately through the posters and also through the visible proofs of his power: the four great fortresses of glittering concrete dominating the ramshackle city, the giant state dwarfing the puny individual. The elegant inscription on the shining tower throws into greater relief the dingy city where, we learn, the giant's captives live in a squalor the more ensconced because they have no standard against which to judge it and no memories of anything better. The hero is deep within enemy territory. The giant, in fact, controls the whole world; there is no region where his writ does not run. Winston sees from his window the investigative helicopters, and they remind him of that far more potent instrument of inquiry and control, the Thought Police. Since this is a technological fairy-tale for the modern age, the hero finds all around him the apparatus of the giant's surveillance system. Victorian children were to be seen and not heard; this oppressor, through his telescreens, both looks and listens. With scarcely any food in the flat, crumbling cigarettes, and a fire-water gin derisively sharing the same ironic name as the broken-down building in which he lives, Winston fixes his face into the mandatory expression of quiet optimism before turning toward the telescreen. The giant must not see his captive's resentment; if he is to be over-come, he must be deceived.

It is instructive to compare Winston with his legendary forerun-ner. Jack is intelligent, intrepid, resourceful, and undaunted. Whether the ogres are cunning or stupid makes no difference; Jack is always too sharp to be bested. He acquires weapons that make him practically invincible: a coat of darkness, a cap that advises him, a sword that severs what it strikes, shoes of swiftness. With such technology, he is ready for any foe. The fable depicts the victory of mind over matter, wit over bulk, intelligence over brute strength; it incarnates Western man's joy in triumphing over seemingly insuperable odds, the triumph of craft and courage over a hostile, overweening nature. The astute hero defeats his more powerful opponents by dint of superior intellect. Invariably in the tale, Jack taunts his enemies before killing them, compelling them before death to confront their folly. He is the trickster, the ironist of his tale, mocking the inept efforts to undo him.

In Orwell's version irony has deserted to the giant: "Here comes a chopper to chop off your head" (p. 175). The concluding line of the nursery rhyme is launched in malicious derision against the bewildered, failed rebel. O'Brien is the ironist of Orwell's tale, and he plays with Winston much as the buoyant Jack plays with his doomed opponents. Jack's trickiest foe is a two-headed Welsh giant, especially malevolent, who seeks his life while pretending to be his friend: the quintessential Englishman (it is the blood of an Englishman that, according to the rhyme, provokes the giant's sadism) faces a Celtic foe. Winston Smith (whose name could not be more English in its tribute to the uncommon Englishman, the great war hero, and to the common Englishman with the most common surname) is deluded by the two-faced O'Brien, who pretends friendship while being the chief Thought Policeman. The name *O'Brien* is as indisputably Irish as *Smith* is English; once again, as in the legend, the most devious and dangerous enemy comes from beyond the English heartland to threaten the English hero.

The parallel is sustained in the battle of wits between Jack and his treacherous enemy. The giant intends to kill Jack while he sleeps. Ever alert, Jack puts an imitation body in the bed and watches, amused, during the night as his dupe smashes it to pieces. Next morning, to the giant's consternation, Jack appears, lightly remarking that his sleep was somewhat disturbed by a rat that gave him two or three slaps of its tail. The casual reference shows that rats hold no more terror for Jack than do giants; Winston, by contrast, is quelled by the irresistible alliance of both.

The final contrast is in our farewells to these characters. The successful Jack is about to marry his princess. He has just accomplished his greatest exploit, penetrating an enchanted castle and liberating many knights and ladies who had been transformed by a sorcerer-giant into perverse, degraded shapes. He finds engraved in large letters on an inner door the secret of the giant's art, plus instructions on how the spell can be broken. Goldstein's book promises to do the same for Winston; in it, the duplicitous O'Brien tells him, he "'will learn the true nature of the society we live in, and the strategy by which we shall destroy it'" (p. 141)—the spell over Oceania and the means to exorcise it.

But where Jack succeeds in restoring the deformed prisoners to their proper shapes, Winston dismally fails. Goldstein's instructions come courtesy of the Giant; the book is a forgery to lead the hero astray. In Orwell's chill revision of the fairy-tale, it is the clever giant who digs hidden pits, the inept hero who blunders into them. At the close the giant's castle is secure as ever; the deformation of human nature proceeds apace. Far from being the savior of others, the hero himself is irrecoverably lost. Instead of success and marriage to a princess, Winston loses everything: Julia, self-respect, belief in truth and love, humanity itself. We take leave of a craven power worshipper, the giant's lover, truckling despicably to the power that has unmanned him. Even the life so shamefully preserved and squalidly possessed will soon be his no more, since, in his odious devotion and abject contrition, he is now in that condition that, in Oceania, certifies one fit for vaporization. Winston is now "cured," which means that there is no longer any reason to keep him alive. We part with a dead man, a corpse waiting to be sent to the grave.

Yet the initial prospects had seemed auspicious. Orwell appears to be maintaining the old dualism of obtuse giant and dexterous hero. Big Brother is apparently a careless, remiss giant. Jack wins in the tale through superior mental agility, and the same felicitous antithesis of nimble hero and ponderous foe seems reassuringly present again. "For some reason" the telescreen in Winston's flat has been placed on the wrong wall (p. 8). The giant has slipped up, as giants always do, and the result is a hidden zone, a blind spot, an alcove from which the prying giant can be excluded. It is the equivalent of Jack's coat of darkness — the power to walk defiantly under the tyrant's nose without being seen. With this guarantee of invisibility and immunity, Winston decides to become a diarist and a criminal. The unusual geography of the room with its misplaced telescreen is his assurance; what Big Brother cannot see, he cannot punish.

True, Winston works for the giant in one of the great fortresses where his job is to ensure his master's infallibility. He is, in addition, fearful and fatalistic. He considers abandoning his plans for a diary (the giant does not like his subjects to have private thoughts or personal records) but goes ahead for the unheroic reason that, diarist or not, the Thought Police will get him just the same. However well one dodges, detection is finally ineluctable. An invincible giant is the axiom from which all Winston's reflections start. His heart quails as he contemplates the Ministry of Truth; it seems impregnable, incapable of being stormed or bombed into submission.

This recalls a passage from an earlier novel, *Coming Up for Air*, where the hero, brooding over the bad times coming, the war that will surely install totalitarianism, is suddenly elated by a vision of indestructible London: "Surely it's too big to be changed? Bound to remain more or less the same." The giant city is simply too huge, too blessedly chaotic, to be tamed to the regimented requirements of the streamlined men; such sprawling vitality cannot be marshaled to the parade ground discipline of totalitarian schemers: "the bombs aren't made that could smash it out of existence" (p. 224). Let the giant's followers do their worst; London is reassuringly indestructible.

Now it is the giant who is indestructible. George Bowling's ecstatic thanksgiving has become in Winston a gloomy capitulation. For Bowling, London's size is a force for good, guaranteeing human survival against totalitarian threat; for Winston, the giant fortress of Minitrue, an enormous pyramid of white concrete soaring skyward, three thousand rooms above ground level and corresponding ramifications below, is a pledge of human defeat, a depressing reminder that Jack is too puny to overthrow this giant. The six-inch tall emperor of Lilliput, drawing his microscopic sword to resist Man-Mountain Gulliver, was not more absurd.[1]

Nevertheless, Winston's defeatism notwithstanding, there is some cause for hope as the story opens. The giant's oversight with regard to the refuge-alcove suggests that his strength perhaps exceeds his intelligence and that the hero can exploit this weakness. Again the hero is so clearly an unwilling servant, blessedly deficient in the sadism that would stigmatize him, like the revolting Syme, as one of the giant's men. Syme is a devotee, a man besotted with destruction, whether of words or people, lingering with dreamy prurience over the obscene details of public hangings. Winston can, admittedly, succumb to psychopathic rage and revel in fantasies of mayhem. The Two Minutes Hate finds him cosseting vivid hallucinations of flogging Julia to death, shooting her full of arrows, raping her, and cutting her throat at the moment of climax. All of this is ominous, considering the carefully nurtured link joining sexual privation, hysteria, and sadism in Oceania; even the hero is not immune. Leaving the antique shop, he meets the girl and, believing her to be a spy, considers following her and crushing her skull with the newly acquired paperweight. (It is heavily ironic that what so attracts Winston to the paperweight is its "uselessness," the fact that it is valuable in itself, not as instrument or utility. Yet within moments of acquiring the beautiful, useless object, he is thinking of turning it into a means of bloody homicide and desisting only because he lacks the energy for the deed.) When Julia's love note reveals her true motive for pursuing him, he eagerly seeks a meeting with her. In the canteen he is elated to see her sitting alone and starts forward to join her, only to be thwarted by an invitation from an inconvenient colleague. To refuse would be too noticeable. Inwardly raging, he sits down at the table, dreaming vengefully of smashing a pickax into the middle of the silly blond face welcoming him.

Yet we are right to refuse to rank Winston alongside Syme and O'Brien as one of the giant's men. Winston is a sinner, but he is not a sadist. That is why he is properly appalled by O'Brien's frightful scenario of humanity's future. When frustrated, he succumbs to frenzy, but he is incapable of Syme's detached delight in torture. Syme's is the pure, impersonal perversion that relishes pain for its own sake, and the victim need not have injured him. He would enjoy crashing the pickax into any face for the sheer fun of it; his is disinterested sadism, a calm connoisseurship in torment. Nor is O'Brien venting a personal frustration when he ecstatically foretells the boot in the face forever.

For him it is a calculated program, not a surrender to rage. The fact that O'Brien rather likes Winston will not deflect him from his impersonal policy of cruelty for cruelty's sake. Syme and O'Brien are the giant's men, and Winston is not of their company.

Undeniable proof is supplied in the incident when the injured Julia deliberately falls on her damaged arm in order to slip the note surreptitiously to Winston. She assumes, rightly, that Winston will come to her assistance. Perhaps she would have been less confident had she known, as we do, what he had been thinking of doing to her when they last met: crushing her skull. Now his enemy lies helpless in agony before him—a delectable prospect for any sadist. Julia's eyes fixed upon his, "with an appealing expression that looked more like fear than pain" (p. 87). It has every luscious component of a sadist's dream: a victim in pain, helpless, above all pleading, because it is the appeal for pity that most excites the sadist, inflaming him to his most ardent efforts.

The effect on Winston is completely opposite. He sees two incompatible things: an enemy bent on destroying him and a fellow creature in agony. Instinctively, as though the pain were his own, he starts forward to help her. It is a high moment in a book not conspicuous for its homage to human nature. We must remember that the love affair is still to come. Winston helps a person in pain, not an attractive woman he hopes to bed, far less a woman he dreams of sharing his life with. Far from lover or wife, she is not even a friend but, in his mistaken view, an enemy hunting his life. Even the Good Samaritan had not had to carry charity so far. It is, properly considered, an inspiring episode in a generally bleak book: the woman deliberately incurring pain as the sole means of revealing love, sufficiently trustful to human nature to believe that the man will help her; the man dismissing all thought of enmity or vengeance to comfort a stricken fellow human being. Such behavior is anathema to the dedicated sadists of Oceania; there is a roar of fury from the telescreen when one prisoner commits the unpardonable sin of helping another. This single episode alone would entitle us to demand Winston's moral extradition from the realm of Big Brother.

But although Winston is unarguably the good man of the book—

superior to the asinine Parsons, the odious Syme, the abstracted Ampleforth, the fanatical O'Brien—one aspect of his personality suggests a disturbing complicity with the evil he opposes. His pessimism and defeatism are weaknesses, undermining his campaign against Big Brother, but in themselves do not impugn his claim to be the giant's foe, working for the tyrant only because there is no alternative. What is disconcerting is his tendency to forget the wickedness of his vocation in the delight of its expertise.

Orwell was reading Conrad during the writing of *Nineteen Eighty-Four* and was doubtless struck by the curiously ambivalent treatment of the accountant whom Marlow meets in the grove of death in *Heart of Darkness*.[2] On the one hand, Conrad's unqualified admiration for work as redemptive—work is not simply good for us; without it we drift, become abandoned and lost—suggests that the chief accountant is exemplary, heroically keeping himself and his books in order even in the grove of death (it is the mess even more than the malice of the place that so sickens Marlow). Yet the accountant's achievement is so clearly an ambiguous one as he complains that the groans of the dying are disturbing his concentration. The self he preserves amid this chaos is less than human, and the triumph over squalor is itself compromised. To enjoy one's work is a blessing, and to strive to do it well is a merit but not when it is at the expense of compassion or truth.

In the perverse world of Oceania the Ministry of Truth is a manufactory of lies. For Winston the assault on truth is Big Brother's worst abomination, and it pains him that Julia can regard it so lightly. Julia, belonging to a younger generation more habituated to the enormities of Ingsoc, cannot understand why Winston should worry so over the mutability of the past and the alteration of records. For Winston (as for his creator) the two greatest evils of our time, especially evil because they are novel, are the growth of power worship and the attack on the concept of objective truth. In our atrocity-drenched century, it is not wars or slavery, death camps or genocide, frightful though they be, that unnerve Orwell so much as the universal mendacity and doublethink of the time. From the millions of corpses littering the age,

Orwell singles out truth as the gravest casualty, the disappearance of the concept of objective truth as even more horrific than the Himalaya of bones. (*CEJL*, 2:478, 3:110). Victims, like the poor, are always with us, but only today is the tyrant secure from reproach as from reprisal, a negative tribute to the skill and zeal of those renegade intellectuals who place their gifts at his service.

Despite his nausea at the distortion of truth, Winston is such a man—a butcher of truth as Syme is a butcher of words. What is far worse, he enjoys doing it. We see him doing the kind of everyday job he performs for Big Brother. Among the standard tasks is one that he puts aside as a kind of treat to be dealt with last. The others are routine lies that any literate person could easily compose, but this one is a challenge to creative mendacity, demanding a skill, even a delight, in lying, which only an accomplished deceiver can command. In another cubicle he sees a rival colleague, engaged, he is convinced, in the same assignment, and he resolves, like any other artist, that his shall be the prize performance. At the end, the hagiography of Comrade Ogilvy completed, he experiences a satisfaction akin to God's when he created Adam. God had dust to start with, but Winston creates from nothing but pure thought. Ex nihil nihil fit. Winston gives the lie to this, and the result is Comrade Ogilvy, a fiction who will henceforth, through Winston's craft, be every bit as real as Charlemagne or Caesar.

It is easy to see why "Winston's greatest pleasure in life was in his work" (p. 38), less easy to forgive it in view of his asseverated detestation of the Ministry of Truth. Plainly he enjoys his work as much as Syme enjoys burking words or Ampleforth finding new rhymes for the "definitive" texts of the great English poets. Amid the admittedly tedious chores, Winston delightedly finds the occasional nugget: "jobs so difficult and intricate that you could lose yourself in them as in the depths of a mathematical problem—delicate pieces of forgery in which you had nothing to guide you except your knowledge of the principles of Ingsoc and your estimate of what the Party wanted you to say. Winston was good at this kind of thing." (p. 38).

Examined closely, the language of this passage is an incriminating giveaway, hurtful to the hero's integrity. Losing oneself in intricate depths is scarcely the way to survive in the devious society of Oceania; it is in Room 101, in the depths of the Ministry of Love, many meters underground, as deep down as it was possible to go, in the intricate mazes, moral and epistemological, of that windowless horror, that Winston finally loses himself forever. *Delicate* sounds complimentary until linked to *forgery,* and to be so well versed in the philosophy of Ingsoc, to know so intuitively what the Party wants, is an inculpation. "Good" is a key concept in this novel. Dickens's Fagin was a good teacher, which is why he was hanged. Winston's diary refers to "one very good one" among the war films he saw at the cinema. There follows a description of various atrocities, some in the mode of comedy—the fat man wallowing in the water like a porpoise before being shot full of holes and sinking beneath waves pink with blood while the cinema audience shouts with laughter; others in a highly technical professional style—"a wonderful shot of a child's arm going up up up right up into the air," tribute to the consummate skill of the cameraman and fully meriting the spontaneous applause of the appreciative spectators (p. 11). It can only be in some equivalent sense that Winston is described as good at his job since his job is to tell lies. O'Brien is a good inquisitor and Room 101 a good torture chamber. Each is good in terms of function, but the function itself is hellish.

Winston's pleasure in solving "tricky" problems has its parallel in Syme's dreamy delectation in destroying words; the human being is lost in the professional. This ability to lose oneself in one's work is startlingly dramatized when the poet Ampleforth, just before his removal to the dreaded Room 101, momentarily forgets his troubles in ecstatic discovery of a piece of useless pedantry connected with his versifying duties. A scholarly joy possesses him as he tells the frightened, indignant Winston the great secret of English poetry: that its whole history has been determined by its lack of rhymes (p. 183). Winston, Syme, and Ampleforth are so enamored of their work, so smitten with the fascination of the difficult—the specialist's occupational hazard—that they miss or ignore its nefarious aims.

To the extent that he enjoys exercising his skill, even when the end product is lies and vaporizations, Winston is an accomplice of the evil he detests. A signal instance of this dissociation is revealed in the debauch of work caused by the sudden switch of alliances during Hate Week. Without even waiting for orders, Winston reports immediately for duty and works almost nonstop for six days to make the necessary falsifications. The work is gargantuan, a six-day decreation to rival God's labors in Genesis. Winston is impressed at the Hate Week rally by the mental athleticism of the little Rumpelstiltskin orator in so dexterously tailoring his speech to fit the new situation. Once again, as in the atrocity films, an admiration for technique prevails over a concern for decency. What Orwell thought of this, the essay on Dali makes plain. (*CEJL*, 3:185–95). The Rumpelstiltskin theme continues in Winston's assignment. The elf's special gift was in knowing how to spin rooms full of straw into gold; Winston similarly tackles mountains of paper as he recycles old lies into new. After a snatch of sleep he crawls back to find yet another deluge of paper demanding his attention; the work is huge, intricate, taxing.

What is intriguing is Winston's anxiety to do a perfect job, despite knowing its immorality. On the sixth day, the negative creation accomplished, he is as fully involved as any other devotee in the sense of self-congratulation that courses through the exhausted, contented Ministry. The deep and secret sigh collectively emitted is part fatigue but equally part recognition of the fact that "a mighty deed" has been achieved, the more striking in that it can never be publicly proclaimed (p. 148). But it is just as irrefutably wicked; some such oxymoron as Milton's "bad eminence" is equally applicable to this achievement.[3] Why is Winston, would-be martyr for immutable truth, dedicated to the concept of an objective external world, so neurotically concerned that these new lies should be undetectable? Boxer in *Animal Farm* works himself to death to strengthen the dictatorship of the pigs, but he is a simpleton who believes in a good Big Brother. Winston has no such excuse for his own exertions; detesting untruth, he strives to devise the most effective lies possible.

This confusion is most apparent when his raging impatience to contact his startling new lover is assuaged by the arrival on his desk of a delicate, difficult piece of work demanding all his concentration.

He has been ordered to falsify a series of production reports in order to discredit a member of the Inner Party due for vaporization. The preoccupied Winston, absorbed in his lies, is happily able to forget Julia for a couple of hours: "this was the kind of thing that Winston was good at" (p. 90).

So much the worse for him. Swift's virtuous horse would have been repelled by such a talent; a proficiency in "saying the thing which is not" is not to be lauded.[4] Winston is an accomplice in murder, but that is not the worst of it, for the horror of Oceania is that one is either victim or accomplice; there is no third option. Yet as Orwell elsewhere reminds us, there is a vital distinction between compulsion and dedication. Against one-eyed fanaticism he recommends a redemptive double vision: "we see the need of engaging in politics while also seeing what a dirty, degrading business it is." Hence his own double attack on idealists and realists alike—the first for childishly believing that every choice is between good and evil, the second for brutally insisting that power is self-justifying and that if a thing is necessary, it is also right. Against dreamers and gangsters alike, Orwell upholds "the saner self that stands aside, records the things that are done and admits their necessity, but refuses to be deceived as to their true nature . . . you also have to keep part of yourself inviolate" (*CEJL*, 4:469–70).

Winston fails to stand aside; he enjoys his murderous employment. Ironically, the task completed, his mind returns to Julia's note, and he experiences an intense desire to stay alive. To live we have to kill. Julia is also a party to murder. How can one live in Oceania and be inviolate? She has participated in countless demonstrations calling for the execution of unknown people for unknown crimes. But she, unlike Winston, has a simple, amoral view of life; her sole aim is to have a good time as often as possible without getting caught. To all else she is indifferent. If the pursuit of the good time entails turning up at public trials to chant for death to the traitors, that is the price one gladly pays. Winston is at once more complex and vulnerable; he seems, at least in part, contaminated by the doublethink he abhors.

Misgivings as to his giant-killing qualifications grow as we read.

By the second diary entry he is despondently concluding that thought-crime is death, a sentiment that O'Brien will later applaud. Yet the key irony is that this pessimist is far too optimistic. "For some reason the telescreen in the living-room was in an unusual position" (p. 8). The words solicit us to believe in chance, coincidence, accident—for *no* reason, is the implication. It is his first blunder. That too convenient alcove where he dreams himself safe is the first of a series of traps into which he stumbles. The fairy-tale promises that intelligence will always master brute strength. Orwell's most unnerving emendation is to make the giant not only strong but clever—far too clever to be outwitted by our best inventions.

Winston in the alcove is fooling only himself; O'Brien has seen through him for seven years. He is also fooling himself when he determines that if he cannot hide his diary, he can at least know if it has been detected. A hair across the book he dismisses as too obvious, preferring, ingeniously, to deposit a grain of dust on the cover, bound to be dislodged if the book is opened. This is the kind of sharpness that serves Jack so well. Winston, unfortunately, is up against a very different kind of giant. "He could at least make sure" (p. 26): even this minimal achievement is beyond him. True, the grain of dust must be dislodged, but it can also be replaced. This giant plays with his foolish adversary; we are reminded of a cat with a mouse, of Hardy's President of the Immortals having his sport with Tess, above all, of Eliot in *The Waste Land*: I will show you fear in a handful of dust.

Winston dismayingly discovers his inferiority as he reflects with shame upon the inept frivolity of his challenge to the Party. For seven years the Thought Police have been watching him like a beetle under a microscope. It is an image straight from that tradition of humiliated man so familiar to us from the pages of Swift and Kafka. The secret rebel has all the while been pathetically transparent, a glass man in a glass house. Without realizing it, he has been conducting a colloquy with the Thought Police when he thought he was soliloquizing. Before the book begins O'Brien has already promised (threatened) a meeting in the place where there is no darkness, and the diary has been written for O'Brien in a far more bitterly ironical sense than Winston ever intended (p. 67). Winston reveals everything, directly or indirectly. He tells his "friend" O'Brien what he will and will not do for the Brotherhood, and O'Brien now knows what Winston loves best in the world. In the room above the antique shop he confesses his horror of rats, and O'Brien now knows what he fears most in the world. Winston helps to prepare his own humiliation in Room 101.

After the exertions of Hate Week, he feels gelatinous with fatigue, his body so drained that he imagines it has become translucent. In fact transparency is his normal condition. Everyone seems able to read his thoughts, and when he is most hidden, he is most exposed. The room where the lovers think to elude surveillance is simply an extension of the alcove fallacy—a sanctuary that is no sanctuary, a private room that is a public stage. Winston and Julia are broadcasting when they think that they are being intimate. His very dreams and nightmares are public property, on file for inspection. O'Brien knows things about Winston that he will not admit to himself and has not only penetrated but solved the nightmare: the identity of the horror behind the wall of blackness that Winston will not acknowledge.

The rebel is really a puppet, and even his acts of resistance are conditioned and sanctioned by a contemptuously omniscient giant. But even before readers realize this, they sense an ambivalence in Winston's attitude toward his foe that augurs ill for the prospect of successful revolt. Even during the detestable Two Minutes Hate, Winston's secret loathing for Big Brother is liable to change disconcertingly into adoration as the tyrant becomes an invincible protector, a rock towering against the hordes of Asia. Jack never shows any tendency to worship his giant. Winston is clearly a compromised man, riven by radically opposed impulses: rebellion versus submission, self-assertion versus self-abasement.

Where Jack is bold and enterprising, Winston is fearful and passive. Always it is the other person—Charrington, Julia, O'Brien—who makes the proposal. Winston is convinced that O'Brien's glance at the end of the Hate is an unmistakable message: there is an underground conspiracy, and O'Brien is in it. But Winston never thinks of acting upon this knowledge. He does not know how, and it would be inconceivably dangerous. The invitation is plain, but he lacks the will, the courage, and know-how to handle it. He knows that O'Brien is an ally who has just made an overture, but this knowledge is inert, barren. Even the decision to open the diary, courageous though it be, confirms his introspective, sedentary nature, his bias toward monologue, his reluctance to engage other people. The momentousness of O'Brien's glance notwithstanding, Winston decides that "that was the end of the story." But for the initiatives of others, he would have remained to the last "in the locked loneliness in which one had to live" (p. 18).

When we ask what Winston is waiting for, the answer is inescapable: he is waiting for O'Brien to contact him. "It had happened at last. The expected message had come. All his life, it seemed to him, he had been waiting for this to happen" (p. 127). Winston's deficiencies are here crystallized. He does not make things happen; they happen to him. He reacts but never initiates. Oceania is, admittedly, a society that inhibits enterprise, but Julia lives there too, and it is she who launches the love affair, plans its progress, and makes all the arrangements up to the decision to rent Charrington's room. Winston, we must conclude, is more immersed in the dependence culture. Writing "Down with Big Brother" in the diary may provide emotional relief but is only marginally superior to babbling it in one's sleep as the fatuous Parsons does; the real question is, How does Winston propose doing it?

Even to ask this question reveals its absurdity. Winston does not even believe he can do it: "The Thought Police would get him just the same" (p. 18). He is the opposite of Jack: fatalistic, despondent, consistently wrong. The frequency of his misjudgments is both staggering and incriminating. "It was always at night—the arrests invariably happened at night. The sudden jerk out of sleep . . . the ring of hard faces round the bed" (pp. 18–19). Once again he is completely mistaken. We (and he) never know when he is arrested—whether at nine in the morning or nine in the evening—but it is not at night or as he predicted. Both he and Julia have risen from bed and dressed themselves; there is no sudden jerk out of sleep. It is almost as if Big Brother derived some perverse pleasure from proving the wiseacre wrong, and it confirms yet again the dispiriting truth of the reconstituted fable: not once throughout does this Jack take the measure of his opponent. Winston should have spent some of the ingenuity he expends on Big Brother's service in protecting himself from error.

He goes wrong from the outset—wrong about Julia whom he instantly dislikes because of her sexual puritanism, "the atmosphere of . . . general clean-mindedness which she managed to carry about with her" (p. 11). *Managed* is the significant word, suggesting something contrived, even rigged, for Julia is a nymphomaniac, adoring (her word) the sexual act in itself, regardless of the partner she performs it with. True, she draws the line at proles—she is a party girl in every sense of the word—but her boast of having slept with hundreds (regretfully scaled down to dozens) indicates that sex is for her what power is for O'Brien: an end in itself, to be avidly pursued for its own sake. The frigid ice maiden who provokes Winston's dislike turns out to be Messalina.

He is equally mistaken about O'Brien, and the narrative style Orwell adopted serves to highlight the intransigence of this self-deception. Orwell employs a mimetic mode in which the hero's mood determines the presentation of event. It is a kind of inverted ventriloquism where the narrator provides a voice for the character's views, surreptitiously surrendering his pen to the deluded protagonist. What is ostensibly rendered as fact is merely mistaken opinion. Winston "knew—yes, he *knew*!" (p. 17) that O'Brien is a fellow dissident. This is really disguised first-person narrative; both italic and exclamation mark are ironic indicators of how thoroughly wrong the judgment is. To err is human, but to do it so consistently and categorically is a reproach to the culprit. Winston takes O'Brien for a freedom fighter; he is in fact Torquemada.

But even Winston cannot avoid occasionally hitting the mark. Brooding upon the fate of his acquaintances, Winston correctly includes the zealot Syme among those marked for destruction. He is acutely prophetic, the more so because he presciently supplies the reason: Syme is too intelligent to survive; he sees too clearly and speaks too plainly. His fanaticism notwithstanding, he is destined for vaporization: "it is written in his face" (p. 45). In fact, Syme is Winston's Baptist, preparing his way in advance; Parsons and Ampleforth are, by contrast, Winston's followers.

Lest we become too impressed by Winston's perspicacity, Orwell immediately appends a series of forecasts that do little credit to the hero's prophetic powers. Mrs. Parsons, O'Brien, and Winston himself are certainties for vaporization, while Parsons and the girl with dark hair (the still-unknown Julia) are equally sure to escape. We never hear what happens to Mrs. Parsons; the only correct prediction concerns himself, and that confirms his defeatism as much as his judgment. "It seemed to him that he knew instinctively who would survive and who would perish" (p. 52). The book does not endorse Winston's dogmatic confidence in his instincts.

The same instincts let him down in the matter of Julia's approach, for he overlooks the straightforward, natural explanation of her behavior. He is petrified in the canteen when he realizes that the girl who sat behind him during the Hate is looking at him now "with curious intensity" (p. 52). He immediately concludes that she is a spy. It is in keeping with his acute self-depreciation—his sensitivity to his meager body, ulcerous leg, false teeth—that he should lack the sexual conceit to interpret this female interest as concupiscence. Since the intensity is not that of desire, it must come from hostility. Accordingly, when Julia slips him the note, he assumes that it must be political—either a fatal summons from the Thought Police or an exciting invitation from the Brotherhood. That it might be a sexual gambit, a solicitation to love, never crosses his mind. For Winston everything is political, and he cannot understand that characters like Julia exist for whom "a good time" is the sole business of life. He sees what is not there: a frigid fanatic eager for his life instead of a randy woman avid for his body.

Yet this ill-founded distrust of Julia coexists with a reckless readiness to trust "old Charrington" (p. 172)—the adjective has as much to do with Winston's condescending affection for the genteel prole as with the antique dealer's age—and this time the mistake is disastrous. Yet what reader is surprised when the sixty-year-old prole is reborn as a thirty-five-year-old Thought Policeman? That Winston trusted him is, in this text, the clearest hint that he is Winston's enemy. The real surprise would have been for Winston to get it right.

A hero diffident to the point of defeatism, consistently and spectacularly mistaken, challenges an omniscient, omnipotent giant. How could the tale end other than it does? The truly interesting, challenging question is, Why does Orwell so shockingly subvert the fable he described as the basic myth of Western man and that he himself so dearly loved as the vindication of his cherished underdog? (*CEJL*, 1:503, 3:22–23, 503).[5] That he does subvert it is incontestable. Winston continues to go astray after his arrest as before it. He wonders whether "they" have got Charrington when in fact Charrington has got him; within seconds Charrington will enter to command the thugs terrifying Winston. He repeats the error when O'Brien enters the cell: "'They've got you too!' he cried" (p. 189). O'Brien's mocking reply shows that duping Winston is all too easy, like taking candy from a child.

Winston is childish: simpleton, *naif, ingénu*. There is a literary tradition in which such characters are shielded and preserved. In certain tales the holy fool survives because God or providence or a good fairy is looking after him. This is the genre taken over and developed by Henry Fielding. Blifil is devious and farseeing, Tom Jones heedless and improvident. But Blifil is bad and Tom good, and that is enough for Fielding: Tom triumphs. Parson Adams is an even purer instance of the type; however gullible, he is in God's (and Fielding's) keeping, and finally no harm can come to him. In other, different tales the hero triumphs through a different set of qualities: courage, resourcefulness, wit—the giant-killer's virtues. Winston is clearly not the latter. His misfortune is to be the *ingénu* at the wrong time in history and literature, at a cultural moment when the concept of the holy fool is obsolete, when God is dead and providence incredible, when might is right and history sides with the big battalions, when trust and a simple heart are a recipe for liquidation. How would Parson Adams fare in Airstrip One? Winston never sees his enemies until they choose to unmask.

Winston's gullibility and obtuseness explain the giant's easy contempt, so profound, indeed, that he insultingly allows Winston to read in the book the following warning: "A Party member lives from birth to death under the eye of the Thought Police. Even when he is alone he can never be sure that he is alone. Wherever he may be, asleep or awake, working or resting, in his bath or in bed, he can be inspected without warning and without knowing that he's being inspected" (pp. 166–167). The irony is that Winston reads this, thinking himself alone and secure. The giant's candor is inseparable from disdain. Winston can be told the truth in the secure knowledge that he will miss it. The contempt is justified: Winston falls asleep, confident of his safety. Meanwhile the Thought Police are on the other side of the wall, about to arrest him as they might have done at their choosing throughout the last seven years. Winston is alseep in every sense of the word.

When he awakes, we see why Charrington was so careful to provide him with an old-fashioned, twelve-hour clock. After his arrest, he cannot, by the clock, determine whether it is morning or evening, he literally does not know the time of day. This has come in modern idiomatic English to describe someone confused and bewildered, living in a dream world, cut off from reality. This window on Winston's befuddlement is crucially important in view of the thoughts he is entertaining just before his arrest. "The future belonged to the proles. . . . Sooner or later it would happen, strength would change into consciousness. . . . In the end their awakening would come" (p. 173).

The position of the proles within *Nineteen Eighty-Four* is so decisive that extended discussion of it will be reserved for a later chapter. Some attempt, however, must be made now to locate them within the giant-hero framework of this argument—in particular what light they throw upon Winston's hope for the overthrow of Big Brother. There is, the text suggests, inside Oceania a giant even more massive and mighty than Big Brother, with the power to defeat the tyrant in any trial of strength; but, tragically, it seems as though the desiderated contest will never take place. The proles are depressingly akin to the conventional giant of fairy-tale: ponderous, irrational, dim, easily duped, and easily led. The adjectives Winston chooses to describe them are revealing: *monstrous, enormous, vast. Enormous* is the word applied to Big Brother's face on the poster and also to the prole couple who almost pulverize Winston in the crush in Victory Square; *monstrous* is used of the menacing Eurasian soldier and also of the prole mother in the backyard of the antique shop (pp. 5, 94, 112, 121).

Clearly an affinity is implied. What these otherwise completely different beings have in common is a stupendous power. But in Big Brother and the soldier the power is malevolently active; in the proles it is either dormant or squandered in trivia. Only in Winston's wishful imagination do the proles appear as a rival power (if there is hope, it is in the proles), for, so far, they have issued no challenge to the giant, and there is no evidence in the text that they ever will. Winston wants it, but in this book that is hardly encouraging. All internal probability suggests that the proles will rest supine forever.

That is certainly the giant's contemptuous assessment. O'Brien scouts a prole rebellion as a preposterous pipe dream that he has helped to concoct. It is part of his malicious plan to dupe the hero, and he himself wrote the perfidious book in which the uprising is forecast: "'The proletarians will never revolt, not in a thousand years or a million. They cannot'" (p. 207). To so categorical, so decisive a dictum, excluding debate or demur, there can only be one of two responses: the speaker is either unopposably right or egregiously wrong. O'Brien is oracle or fathead. Either the decision to ignore the proles, to let them run free like wild animals, is a blunder of the first magnitude, or it is justified in terms of the book we have read. The text gives us no right to believe that O'Brien is a fool or that the Party has miscalculated. What we choose to believe outside the text is our own business, to which *Nineteen Eighty-Four* may not dictate, but there is a reciprocal obligation: we must not coerce the text into gratifying our political predilections.

Nineteen Eighty-Four is a work of literature, not of politics. We must assay Winston's anticipations of a prole rebellion within their fictional matrix. Why should Winston, so consistently wrong throughout, suddenly be right now? Why should we believe his predictions about the distant future when he does not know what time it is today? The literary truth is that Winston does not inspire confidence as prophet or sage. The only readers who will agree with him are those prepared to bully the text into echoing their own desires. It is surely significant that in almost the same breath as the prole prediction, Winston should err yet again in referring to "'the thrush that sang to us.'" Julia rebukes this anthropocentric delusion: "'He was singing to please himself. Not even that. He was just singing'" (p. 174).

Equally significant is the fact that two of his most potent symbols—the prole mother and the paperweight—should be depreciated at the moment of arrest. The singing abruptly stops; Winston hears the washtub being flung across the yard, the woman's angry protest, a yell of pain, and then silence. This is followed by the smashing of the paperweight. The fragment of coral rolls across the floor: "How small, thought Winston, how small it always was!" (p. 175). The exclamation mark records the shock of the discovery, but Winston was alone in ever thinking it impregnable. He has in fact been seduced by the paperweight even more than by the woman. Gazing fascinated into its interior, he had dreamed it to be a separate world, self-contained and transcendent, a refuge from the malice of Big Brother. The irresistible vision of the gleaming paperweight on the gateleg table is decisive in tempting him to rent the room: "The paperweight was the room he was in, and the coral was Julia's life and his own, fixed in a sort of eternity at the heart of the crystal" (p. 120).

It is an image as beautiful as any metaphysical conceit, but, however beautiful, it is a delusion. The room and its contents, paperweight included, are the property of the Thought Police. They lurk behind the treasured steel engraving; there is a rat hole in Eden. There is no private, secure world to which the lovers can make their inner emigration; the only eternity is a boot in the face forever. The room is in Oceania as Winston's mind is in O'Brien's: contained, subordinate. Evil is not, as it is for Dante or Milton, circumscribed by good; good lives its brief, fragile period within a matrix of omnipotent evil. The paperweight will survive for just so long as some uniformed thug chooses to let it. The external evil world can break into the idyll at will.

Winston's blunders about room and paperweight simply confirm our impression of a contest between an erring individual and a Party farseeing and devious. Part Three, the sequel to the arrest, dramatizes the threefold victory—moral, intellectual, and physical—won by the giant over Winston. The moral defeat occurs when O'Brien plays back the incriminating tape of the atrocities Winston has sworn to commit, the physical when he compels Winston to confront his own vileness in the mirror. (These will be analyzed in chapter 6. This chapter will concentrate on the systematic intellectual demolition of Winston as the shame of his mental inferiority is forced upon him.)

O'Brien's aim is to make Winston despise himself; the giant is resolved not to kill Jack until the hero becomes his worshipper. The two chief strategies of humiliating a man are to show him his folly or his corruption, and both are employed. "He did not know where he was" (p. 179): this opening sentence of Part Three has an underlying meaning that transcends its immediate application. Orwell is not merely referring to the place of imprisonment. Did Winston ever know where he was? Was he not always a prisoner without knowing it? When the guard laughs down on Winston's contortions after striking him, he is simply following his master's lead, for we now know that Big Brother's attitude to Winston has been from the outset one of derisive disdain. And with justice—Winston is a poor opponent intellectually. Despite his comforting belief that "they could spy upon you night and day, but if you kept your head you could still outwit them," (p. 135), the text reveals O'Brien's altogether too easy access to the few cubic centimeters within Winston's skull. O'Brien's ability to read Winston's thoughts is recognized by Winston himself from the opening pages. It is just that Winston misconstrues inquisition as sympathy: "don't worry, I am on your side!" (p. 17). Winston is right about O'Brien's insight into his mind; it is concerning his motive that he goes so damagingly astray. Winston does not keep his head. It is as much O'Brien's possession as it is his own.

Winston is repeatedly unnerved to find that even his secret arguments and hidden consolations are anticipated and rebutted by his adversary. He wonders bitterly why he should be tortured and degraded when the final result is, in any case, a foregone conclusion;

O'Brien answers the unspoken objection as though it had been uttered aloud. Looking at the power worshipper's face, Winston is suddenly struck and heartened by its tired, aging appearance. O'Brien too is a dead man, as much as Winston a corpse awaiting delivery to the grave. Winston's comfort is as instantly cancelled when O'Brien telepathically expresses his awareness of mortality and his strategy for handling it: "'You are thinking . . . that my face is old and tired,'" but "'the weariness of the cell is the vigour of the organism'" (p. 209). This problem of personal extinction is, we shall see in chapter 5, a crucially important subtext in *Nineteen Eighty-Four*. For the moment it suffices to point out that once again O'Brien knows Winston's unuttered thoughts, exhibiting a godlike omniscience that the giant of fairy-tale blessedly lacked.

The insistence upon O'Brien's omniscience becomes, indeed, otiose, even irritating; is it necessary to keep telling us what we now know? Orwell apparently thinks it is. When O'Brien provocatively upholds Ptolemy against Copernicus, insisting that the earth is at the center circled by the sun, Winston convulsively moves but says nothing. O'Brien continues as though answering a remonstration and proceeds to make mincemeat of the counterarguments that Winston is privately entertaining. It must be very frustrating to dispute with someone who simultaneously knows every argument you have before you make it and its devastating refutation.

Such a debate can only have one conclusion. No wonder that Winston comes to feel that O'Brien's mind contains his own, that mentally as well as physically he is a pygmy before this colossus, absolutely outmatched in mind as well as body. No wonder too that when O'Brien is not being fanatical, he should be mockingly ironical, for he knows that the contest is a walkover. Invited to ask any question he will, Winston battles to hold back the one that is causing him greatest anxiety and is finally precipitated into voicing it by the amusement on O'Brien's face, the ironical gleam that even his spectacles seem to emit. O'Brien, Winston suddenly realizes, is amused because he knows the question that Winston longs to ask yet dares not. The realization that he is being tormented serves to make the anguish greater as the sadist coyly responds: "'You know what is in Room 101. . . . Everyone knows what is in Room 101'" (p. 206). It is the same stonewalling reply that Iago makes to the distraught Othello—"what you know you know"—and it leaves Winston as confused and stricken as Shakespeare's bewildered hero.[6]

The climactic demonstration of O'Brien's telepathic powers occurs just before he sends Winston to Room 101. Alone in his cell, Winston is pondering his true feelings toward Big Brother. He has been devising how to dupe the tyrant by concealing his hatred until that split second of execution when he will have misled his enemy into killing a man who is still a rebel. He is savoring in anticipation the vindictive elation of that moment when O'Brien enters the cell. For the last, decisive time Winston has been outthought and outmaneuvered. O'Brien contemns the stupid attempt to deceive him; Winston is a thought criminal whose thoughts are as visible as his features. O'Brien knows that Winston has been thinking about Big Brother and demands the truth of these thoughts by laying claim to the power of God: "'no lies—you know that I am always able to detect a lie'" (p. 224). It is a breathtaking claim that would be derisory, arrogant, and outrageous were it not undeniably true.

As a contest it has been laughably unequal, as grotesquely mismatched as any contest can be when one participant is omniscient and the other a dunce. Not once does O'Brien fail to read Winston; not once does Winston anticipate his foe. He is forever being surprised by O'Brien, and the shocking metamorphosis of friend into persecutor does nothing to alter this. He is surprised when O'Brien first accosts him, surprised when he turns off the telescreen, surprised when he enters the cell: "'They've got you too!'" Even as explicit enemy O'Brien retains this power to startle. A signal instance occurs when he invites Winston to submit his explanation of the Party's lust for power, to transcend the "how" of Oceania and lay bare the "why."

A stale weariness possesses Winston as he distastefully contemplates the batch of clichés that O'Brien so obviously demands. All those ancient, moth-eaten arguments given classic expression by Dostoyevsky's Grand Inquisitor: that men are weak and corrupt and must be disciplined for their own sakes, that the choice is between a ruinous freedom and programmed happiness, that the dictator reluctantly assumes the depleting burden of power as a savior of men, that power is merely a means to an end, that the greatest good of the greatest number is the overriding rule. Wearily Winston begins to parrot the tiresome old prospectus that he is so sure O'Brien has solicited. He is at once punished for his egregious blunder. O'Brien does not, of course, want Winston to be his equal in insight, for where, then, would his superiority lie? But neither can he abide such crass ignorance; the adversary must have some intelligence if he is to be worth overcoming. Winston's impercipience deserves chastisement. And yet it is merely a heightened instance of the hero's habitual incomprehension.

It is worth pausing to ask why O'Brien should rage so fiercely against Winston for trying to supply a rational justification for Ingsoc or why he should so violently, so pathologically, proclaim its pure irrationalism. It is the more important to answer this in view of certain mistaken objections to this aspect of Orwell's book. The most notorious of these is Deutscher's charge about "mysticism of cruelty," Orwell's alleged surrender to sadomasochistic impulses within himself which he neurotically projected onto an innocent external world.[7] The same criticism has been more temperately but just as damagingly put: "There is absolutely no point in governing through pain when it is so much easier and less stressful to govern through pleasure. Ultimately, *Brave New World* is a much more accurate picture of a predictable future than *1984*."[8] Man is headed for a demeaning pleasure park rather than for Room 101.

This completely overlooks the fact that the giant in fairy-tale always rules, always chooses to rule, through terror—and not just in fairy-tale. Machiavelli, pointing out that men must be either pampered or crushed, wheedled or destroyed, that armed prophets conquer and unarmed prophets come to grief, poses the question whether it is better to be loved than feared or the reverse. He answers that it is far better to be feared than loved if one cannot ideally be both. This is because "men worry less about doing an injury to one who makes himself loved than to one who makes himself feared. The bond of love is one which men, wretched creatures that they are, break when it is to their advantage to do so but fear is strengthened by a dread of punishment which is always effective."[9] Nietzsche too comes down decisively on the side of force as the overriding element in human relations: "To expect that strength will not manifest itself as strength, as the desire to overcome . . . is every bit as absurd as to expect that weakness will manifest itself as strength. A quantum of strength is equivalent to a quantum of will, urge, activity."[10] Isabella in *Measure for Measure* utters her fervent appeal for compassion:

> O, 'tis excellent
> To have a giant's strength, but it is tyrannous
> To use it like a giant.[11]

Then what, asks Nietzsche derisively, is the point of having it?

Pareto, a major intellectual contributor to the rise of fascism, declared that societies are characterized above all by the nature of their governing elites and, following Machiavelli, argued that the few can rule the many by resorting to one of two methods: force and guile. Clearly he has in mind Machiavelli's famous antithesis between the lion and the fox. Political elites divide naturally into two families—the family of the lions and the family of the foxes—exhibiting a preference for either brutality or cunning, terror or deceit.[12] In the Ministry of Love O'Brien rapturously proclaims the regime of Big Brother to be the most consummate example imaginable, the paradigm and nonpareil, of a lion elite. Such a beast cannot live without blood. Without the adversary, Big Brother loses his own raison d'être; like Voltaire's God, if the adversary did not exist, he would have to be invented.[13] The giant needs and wants Jack, an endless succession of Jacks, for what good is it to have power and no opportunity to use it? A giant who wants a quiet, tranquil life, with nobody challenging or resisting, might as well not be a giant—will indeed, if Pareto's analysis is correct, soon cease to be one. This is what lies behind Pareto's celebrated aphorism that history is a graveyard of aristocracies. According to Pareto those aristocracies that grow moderate will fall, victims of their own weakness, to be swept away and replaced by a new, violent elite. That O'Brien has read Pareto is made clear in Goldstein's book. The caution against becoming too soft has been thoroughly heeded; this is one giant who will never fall through a lack of cruelty.

Hence the studied sadism, the programmatic terror, of the whole Miniluv section is far from being excessive; it is essential to the system of Oceania. Winston's sense of inferiority deepens with the regularity and severity of his defeats. The man who never wins comes to see himself as a loser, his conqueror as a superior being, perhaps even a god. "O'Brien was a being in all ways larger than himself. There was no idea that he had ever had, or could have, that O'Brien had not long ago known, examined and rejected. His mind contained Winston's mind" (p. 203). It would be a blunder to believe that this self-abasement stems simply from the fact that Winston is strapped to a table while O'Brien controls the dials of torture. The homage expressed is clearly paid to the mental rather than the physical giant. Intellectual authority has gone to live with brute power, the nightmare that Orwell most feared. Prometheus concedes Zeus's omnipotence but denies that might is right. Winston is, in the end, a broken Prometheus.

The danger signs are there from the beginning. Long before Winston knows O'Brien's true identity, he is ominously inclined to self-prostration before the demigod. It is not to the Thought Policeman but to Goldstein's heroic lieutenant that "a wave of admiration, almost of worship, flowed out from Winston . . . it was impossible to believe that he could be defeated. There was no stratagem he was not equal to, no danger that he could not foresee. Even Julia seemed to be impressed" (p. 142). And with good cause: O'Brien is impressive. Nevertheless that strategically situated *even* tells us that it is Winston who is most at risk, and when the insurgent becomes the inquisitor, he remains superman, and the outlook for resistance is bleak. "O'Brien knew everything. A thousand times better than Winston he knew what the world was like" (p. 208). O'Brien is now the enemy, but the adulation remains constant. It is to his cognitive powers even more than his physical prowess or control of the instruments of pain that

Winston submits, and such craven deference is a sure recipe for eventual surrender. Jack learns to worship the giant, and not just for being big but for being right.

It is Winston's mental impotence even more than his corporeal helplessness that makes the transactions of Miniluv so dispiriting to read. The little man is so repeatedly, monotonously bested. He shrinks back in his bed; "whatever he said, the swift answer crushed him like a bludgeon"; "as usual, the voice had battered Winston into helplessness" (pp. 211, 213). O'Brien wins every argument and would do so even were Winston not his prisoner. Winston is left with only a logicless, emotional detestation of the reasoning he cannot refute: "Feebly, without arguments, with nothing to support him except his inarticulate horror of what O'Brien had said, he returned to the attack" (p. 213). Winston may be a desponder, but he is no coward, he deserves credit for holding out, but it is a rearguard action, doomed and futile. "How easy it all was! Only surrender, and everything else followed" (p. 220). True, it takes Room 101 to complete this capitulation, but the hero of the fairy-tale had never hosted such a sad speculation. "They can't get inside you" (pp. 135, 230): acknowledging the certitude of capture and execution, the lovers console themselves with this seemingly irrefutable truth. The book, however, upholds O'Brien as its true prophet. He foretells what Winston will become: the contrite ex-heretic, "'utterly penitent, saved from himself, crawling to our feet of his own accord." Momentarily Winston may be appalled by the world of Big Brother, "'but in the end you will do more than understand it. You will accept it, welcome it, become part of it." Winston's response is pitifully inadequate; all he can do is protest weakly, "'You can't!'" (p. 213). This is little more than an emotional reflex, a petulant wail that what he does not like cannot occur. In this book such childish expostulation is no defense.

Despite all this, we must be fair to Winston, the more so because, as I shall later argue, many critics have been too severe, pillorying him as though he were singularly culpable, exceptionally recreant to some common standard of decent conduct easily available to the average human being. In *Nineteen Eighty-Four* Winston is superior to the average human being. He avoids sadism, no small achievement in Oceania. He is not, despite repeated humiliations from O'Brien, a quitter—not, at least, until the final, unendurable trial in Room 101. He is undeniably the best man in the book. He is, moreover, a good man; the tragedy (and it is a representative, not a unique, tragedy) is that, finally, he is not good enough. The reader would do well, however, to avoid any pharisaical rush to judgment on Winston's deplorable insufficiency, would be better advised to remember the words of Nathan to David: thou art the man. A proper reading requires that we see Winston not as some flagrant example of untoward weakness but, like a negative Crusoe, as the everyday human representative, his faults those of mankind.

This understanding, however, does not prevent us from wishing that he were not so easily caught off guard. After the appalling mirror episode there is a rally: "He was much better. He was growing fatter and stronger every day" (p. 218). This physical improvement is a direct consequence of the much better treatment he receives; he is fed and washed regularly, given a change of clothing, provided with new false teeth. To what purpose? he might have asked himself. Even the most gullible man could not believe that Torquemada has turned humanitarian, that the sadists have become kind. His previous experience might have alerted him to the technique employed by the Thought Police of sadistically building people up to make their fall the greater, just as they did before his arrest. Winston, deludedly secure in a hiding place that is nothing of the kind, is lured into thinking that all is well. The result is a striking physical improvement. He puts on weight; he no longer needs gin to see him through the day; his ulcer subsides; his coughing fits end.

It is a trap. The Thought Police survey the improvement, maliciously anticipating his reduction to a bag of filth. Despite the pattern being repeated, Winston falls once again into the same snare. As he recovers in his cell, he begins to grow proud of his body, a remarkable development when we remember his previous shame (he had had to nerve himself to strip naked before Julia). It is all too easy to see why, after the mirror humiliation, he should rejoice in what had formerly been an embarrassment; unprepossessing though he is, he is no longer the bag of filth, and that alone is cause for celebration.

Yet such pride is dangerous, and he should have been more suspicious concerning his captors' generosity. Pride goes before a fall, and Winston, failing to learn from experience, suffers the ultimate, irredeemable fall. Part Three is a more shocking recapitulation of the catastrophe that concludes Part Two, with the debacle of Room 101 complementing the arrest in the antique shop. The book ends with the depressing coda of inanition in the Chestnut Tree. We leave Winston gazing into not the paperweight but the gin glass; gin has become "the element he swam in . . . his life, his death and his resurrection." The waiters treat him as a fixture: "there was no need to give orders. They knew his habits" (p. 229). He is a ruined man, so much a wreck that the giant can ignore him to seek out new foes, secure in the knowledge that he no longer matters. From giant-killer to giant-lover: there has been no more dispiriting transformation in modern literature.

5

THE SAVAGE GOD

Nineteen Eighty-Four is about love in our time, its present status and future prospects. Love is notoriously multiform, and the text covers every conceivable variation: sacred and profane, spiritual and carnal, marital and adulterous, sacrificial and exploitative, *caritas* and eros. Like *Paradise Lost* it is at once a love story and an account of man's relationship to God, a love story conducted against the background of a rebellion against God. The theme of love predominates throughout—from the naming of the Ministry of Love to the consummation of the affair between Winston and Big Brother. It contains all the timeworn elements of the great affairs of legend and literature: passion, infidelity, contrition, the blissful return to the loving breast so wilfully, so wantonly, slighted.

The first diary entry announces the book's major contest: love as compassion versus love as power worship, a delight in atrocity for its own sake. Winston records the futile devotion of the lifeboat-woman, vainly (and, for the spectators, hilariously) interposing her body as an absurd shield between the child and the bullets. He thinks she is a Jewess; she is certainly spiritually related to Jesus who said that the greatest love is to die for another and showed us how to do it.

Terrified, "blue with fright herself" (p. 10), she overcomes this in her beautiful, useless act of self-sacrifice. The passage is proleptic of much that is to come: the blue, protruding tongues of the hanged prisoners that so enchant Syme; the scared child "burrowing" into the woman's breast, so different from the rats that will, as O'Brien promises, burrow into Winston; the chill contrast between heroic selflessness and the sickening self-preservation in Room 101.

But for Winston it is a reminder of things past, of the equally futile gesture of comfort enacted by his mother when she pressed the dying child to her breast. The act is morally what the paperweight is aesthetically: "useless," nonproductive, bearing no practical fruit or quantifiable utility. It is simply good in itself, regardless of consequence. Winston cherishes it as the human act—the hallmark of a certain concept of human nature, once an accepted moral ideal and now almost obsolete and doomed to extinction in Oceania. It is the love of the weak for the weaker, the compassion of the condemned for their fellow victims, in stark contrast to that other love exhibited in the text: the love of the weak for the strong, that prostration before power first seen in the collapse of the woman at the end of the Hate, head buried in prayer, lips tremulously murmuring, "'My Saviour!'" (p. 16).

All these varieties of love—the love of God and of man, Winston's love (or loves) for Julia and Julia's for him, Winston's love for O'Brien and for Big Brother, O'Brien's love of power, maternal love, the love of 2713 Bumstead J., that improbable Good Samaritan, for his starving brother, the love of the terrified Jewess for the terrified child—demand our appraisal and response. Behind all of this is *Paradise Lost,* that archetypal story of sinful lovers and an angry God, but it is Orwell's adaptation of Milton's tale to the altered circumstances of modern man that provides the essential clue to the innermost meaning of his own text.

In *Paradise Lost* human love begins as wedded purity, declines into debauched self-gratification, and is finally restored to its former sinlessness but with the addition of a melancholic maturity appropriate to the post-Edenic world: the loving compassion of each fallen partner for the other. Orwell's love affair moves through a different set of changes to a radically different resolution. It begins for Winston as a fantasy of vengeance—sadistic retaliation against the Party's puritanism. Admittedly this occurs during the Hate, when his dislike for nearly all women, especially those young and pretty, plumbs psychopathic intensity: what we cannot have we easily hate.

When he discovers the incredible truth of Julia's desire, the murderousness fades from his longings. Julia becomes simply an attractive woman whom he wants to sleep with and who, amazingly, wants to sleep with him. Far from resenting her promiscuity, he welcomes it as injecting extra spice into the copulation. He is not just bedding a desirable girl; he is defying the Party. Just like the heroes of Restoration comedy who seem to enjoy deceiving husbands even more than fornicating with their wives, so Winston gets more pleasure from cheating Big Brother than from mounting Julia. The Party has politicized the whole of life, deforming sexuality with everything else. Private emotions are no more immune to Ingsoc than private rooms are barred to telescreens. In the old, prerevolution days the unavailing signs of love had once made human sense but not now. The abolition of *caritas*, of the compassion so touchingly demonstrated in the gestures of the doomed women toward the doomed children, is paralleled in the degradation of eros. Once a man could look at the naked body of an attractive woman and experience only pure lust, unblemished desire. But human nature has changed, has been changed, and even those who deplore the transformation are implicated in it: "No emotion was pure, because everything was mixed up with fear and hatred" (p. 104). Sexual desire is contaminated by political passion.

The relationship quickly shifts, however, from political promiscuity to an everyday affair. Winston forgets Big Brother and delights in Julia as a desirable sex object. Finally there is a startling modulation into full-blown love, married love, in which the participants give as well as take. Julia is no longer just a pleasurable means of defying Big Brother or even a delectable female body but a person in her own right, with all the dignity that this implies. "Hail, wedded love": Milton's great hymn to hymeneal bliss becomes appropriate, for it is now a marriage.[1] That the Party will never sanction it is the clinching proof of its sanctity, for the Party's marriages are a depravation.

Winston begins as political adulterer (at the first orgasm he is thinking of Big Brother), moves to self-centered opportunist, and graduates to husband. "Not merely the love of one person, but the animal instinct, the simple undifferentiated desire: that was the force that would tear the Party to pieces" (p. 103). He finds, initially, political comfort in Julia's promiscuity. It sounds like still more wish fulfillment. If the simple animal desire by itself can overturn the state, why haven't the proles done so? Winston's reflections are not about simple sex at all but about sex as insurrection—a highly sophisticated speculation beyond the reach of any animal or any prole. As he looks at the sleeping woman he has just possessed, we sense a different attitude, "a pitying, protecting feeling," a tenderness that is closer to the lifeboat-woman's compassion than to the mindless drive of an animal. Already he is on the path that will take him from "the simple undifferentiated desire" to "the love of one person" (p. 103).

Julia hates the Party for the unpolitical reason that it stands between her and the good time that is her motive for living. She at first sees Winston as a means to an end, a device for the good time, with no more personal dignity than a dildo. Yet within weeks of the first encounter they have committed the unspeakable folly of renting Charrington's room. The reason is astounding, considering their initial motives for launching into the affair. They want the room not for short sex but for long love, not as "a fine and private place" for coupling but as a home for lovemaking in the widest sense. Winston had thought of renting the room even before he learns that Julia loves him, but the aim then was to be a solitary Adam in an isolated Eden. Now it is Adam and Eve who want the room, not just for convenient copulation but to be together.

Winston is now thinking like a married man and a married man of some duration rather than a bridegroom still aglow with the ardor of the honeymoon: "He wished above all that they had some place where they could be alone together *without* feeling the obligation to make love every time they met" (p. 114). Could there be a better definition of married domesticity? Politics cedes to eroticism, and then eroticism is elevated to married love. They are now, in effect, a married couple, old-fashioned and traditional, equipped with all the customary domestic accoutrements: antique double bed (only the proles now use them), gateleg table, muslin curtains, outmoded twelve-hour clock, paperweight, all that is missing is Gordon Comstock's aspidistra. Privacy is their pursuit—not the privacy of the adulterous but the privacy of the married. In the yard below their window, like another household fixture, is the prole mother, singing trite, sentimental songs that she somehow almost ennobles, forever washing clothes and pegging diapers on a line. What drives Emma Bovary crazy is what these lovers pine for: the banality of married life.

Yet they know too that this is deliberately hastening their advent in that rival structure, the Ministry of Love. Folly three times over, a lunatic project, an unconcealable crime: these are the terms in which Winston judges their action. If we ask why they consciously take so insensate a step, there is only one answer: "The temptation of having a hiding-place that was truly their own, indoors and near at hand, had been too much for both of them" (p. 113). They are overwhelmed by love, an improbable Oceanic Romeo and Juliet, with none of the obvious glamor or romance. Yet below the inauspicious surface there is something poignantly romantic in this unprepossessing pair—the thirty-nine-year-old truth distorter with the varicose ulcer and the twenty-six-year-old nymphomaniac from the fiction department—making their doomed commitment to each other.

What precipitates the "lunatic" decision to rent the room is the mutual disappointment experienced when Julia's menstrual period begins early and ruins the planned return to the Golden Country. Winston's instantaneous reaction is a violent anger, a sense of being cheated out of something he has come to regard as his due. This rage at being bilked comes while they are in a crowd of people. In the crush their hands accidentally meet: "She gave the tips of his fingers a quick squeeze that seemed to invite not desire but affection" (p. 114). This is not the lustful act of the sexually voracious woman but the sympathetic gesture of the loving wife, wordlessly commiserating with her downcast husband and assuring him that, setback notwithstanding, all will be well. And it works. Winston is visited by the stoic insight that this must be a standard, recurring disappointment of married life, "and a deep tenderness, such as he had not felt for her before, suddenly took hold of him" (p. 114). The petulant, spoiled child is transformed into the understanding, forbearing adult. Far from being soured against marriage, he wishes that they were a married couple of ten years' standing. The ambition is so incredibly modest: to be Gordon Comstock or George Bowling, to live with one woman, to walk through the streets with her talking trivialities, to buy odds and ends for the house with her. It is a measure of the frighteningly strange country this modern Gulliver lives in, more lunatic than Laputa and infinitely more perilous, that so tame an aspiration should be about as sensible as bathing in a piranha-infested stream.

Extolling the genius of Joyce, Orwell described him as a literary Columbus, discovering what had been there all the time under everyone's nose (*CEJL*, 1:543). The wonder of the everyday, the treasure hidden in the mundane, is indeed the triumph of a work like *Ulysses*. Something similar manifests itself in the marital idyll of *Nineteen Eighty-Four*. Lying in bed beside the sleeping woman, Winston wonders how at any time "in the abolished past" the miracle of love could ever have been normal, routine, ordinary (p. 117). *Ulysses* is a text consecrated to ordinary miracles, everyday epiphanies. In *Nineteen Eighty-Four*, by contrast, life is routinely hellish, love a transient miracle fragile as the paperweight. Winston's fantasy is to perpetuate the miracle; his meditation on the paperweight is an attempt to remove the room, with all its domestic detail and its aura of abiding marriage, out of the nightmare into the humdrum eternity of the glass circumference.

Despite ramshackle furniture and bug-infested bed, despite the squalor of the surrounding slum, the lovers are, like our first parents, in Eden: "dirty or clean, the room was paradise" (p. 122). Even Satan can sometimes speak true:

> The mind is its own place, and in itself
> Can make a Heaven of Hell, a Hell of Heaven.[2]

Winston and Julia are in heaven. Marriage agrees with him. His physical and mental health improve; he forsakes gin and no longer feels impelled to make faces at the telescreen or curse at the top of his voice. Crucial to this psychological resurrection is the room, an inviolate, alternative world, "a pocket of the past where extinct animals could walk" (p. 122). Among the resuscitated species are married lovers.

Yet in their bones each knows that the room is far from inviolate and that capture is inevitable. They continue to nourish impractical dreams—securing Party approval for their marriage, disappearing to begin a new life as proles, becoming partners in a suicide pact—but never once countenance a prospect of separation. Till death us do part: the pledge is embraced, albeit unofficially. Rationally each knows that "the best thing for us" would be to abandon the room and never meet again" before it's too late" (p. 134). It already is too late, for the land-lord is a Thought Policeman, but, unaware of this, they still believe they can choose safety. Winston tells Julia that she could, if prudent, live for another half-century. The girl who initially reveals herself to Winston is concerned above all with two things: self-preservation and self-gratification. She rejoices that her first lover killed himself before he could betray her; there is no pity for the dead man, simply relief that her own skin was saved. Yet now she condemns that skin to certain torture rather than leave Winston. She rejects his sensible advice: "'what you do, I'm going to do'" (p. 135)—another echo of the marriage vow, of a commitment for good or for ill. The language used by these lovers is, naturally, not the exalted, breath-catching idiom of the great lovers of literature—how could it be in the deliberately diminished and degraded world of Oceania, bent upon extirpating every noble sentiment with every high emotion?—but their devotion to each other is as total and unqualified as that of their illustrious predecessors.

It is, significantly, Julia, sex-mad devotee of the good time, who becomes the leader in love, raising Winston by example to her own high level of unconditional fidelity. Winston, accepting the phony invitation to uplift the Newspeak dictionary, takes Julia along to O'Brien's apartment for no other reason than that he can no longer imagine a life without her or contemplate any action that does not include her. She has no role to play there except as Winston's wife, and in fact O'Brien insultingly treats her as a wife of a very old-fashioned type whose husband can be presumed to speak for her. Dickens's Mr. Bumble castigates the law as an ass for supposing that a wife acts under the husband's discretion, but O'Brien (like the law, also a bachelor) makes the same disparaging assumption.[3] Her inferiority is made plain in the preliminary command that she must be first to leave. From then on she is ignored, sitting disregarded throughout the male conversation.

Yet the climax of the scene occurs when the woman shatters this male monopoly, and she does so in the name and defense of love. O'Brien has been catechizing Winston on his willingness to obey the Brotherhood, obtaining to each solicitation to atrocity an instantaneous assent. When, with the final, searching question, he asks if they are prepared to part forever, Julia, unwilling to trust the man to answer for both, disrupts the male decorum of the interview: "'No!'" broke in Julia" (p. 140). Equally revealing are the intrusive verb, the curt, one-word reply, and the exclamation mark, all indicating the vehemence, the categorical dismissal, of the very thought of separation. As well ask Desdemona to divorce Othello.

The woman's love is greater than the man's, Julia's refusal is instinctive and immediate. Winston is slower and less decisive, and his delay suggests a conflict between powerful competing desires: the delectable prospect of toppling Big Brother versus the bliss of lifelong union with Julia. Does he hate Big Brother more than he loves Julia? For a time it seems touch and go. He struggles to answer, and only when he hears the word does he know his own decision: "'No' he said finally" (p. 140)—without an exclamation mark. It could so easily have gone the other way. Still the decision is made; the husband triumphs over the terrorist, the lover over the politician. Winston's love for Julia is greater than anything else, including the tyrant's downfall. "Down with Big Brother," he had written voluptuously in his diary, realizing only later what his deepest mind had transmitted to the fingers holding the pen. But that was before Julia. He still yearns for that downfall—how much the catechism of agreed atrocities makes chillingly clear—but not if it means losing his beloved; that price is too high.

If there is no equivalent struggle in Julia, that is because she is not concerned with Big Brother's overthrow and cannot credit it. How to evade, not how to abolish, him is her endeavor, and until now she has concentrated on circumventing the restrictions against a good time. Now love has replaced sex as the only thing that matters. To understand this Julia, we need only recall Byron's heroine of the same name in *Don Juan,* sacrificing all for love and explaining why she will not regret what has cost her so dear:

> Man's love is of his life a thing apart,
> 'Tis woman's whole existence.[4]

Those women who regard this as the most notorious piece of offensive condescension ever penned by a man on the subject of heterosexual love will probably consider *Nineteen Eighty-Four* as running it a close second.

Even the naming of the characters is instructive. The hero (for obvious reasons) is alone in possessing the two names normally given to Western people. (Admittedly we learn that Parsons is called Tom, but that is an accident, a piece of information casually disclosed by his wife in conversation with Winston) (p. 20). Otherwise the male characters have surnames only. Goldstein (Trotsky's real name was Bronstein) is a stereotype of the dissident Jewish intellectual, the eternal troublemaker. O'Brien's name in this Swiftian book suggests an inversion of norms, as the quintessential Englishman is mastered by an Irish-named opponent, much as in *Gulliver's Travels* Swift took pleasure in making horses superior to men. The Catholic name too sits well with the devout exponent of the new religion. Syme, Ampleforth, Charrington, Wilsher, Tillotson, Ogilvy: none has a Christian name in this distinctly un-Christian text.

Julia by contrast has no surname. Waking after the first lovemaking, it occurs to Winston that he still does not know her surname, and the thought recurs when they part. If he ever did discover it, he keeps it to himself; the reader knows her only as Julia to the book's end. She is, in fact, Winston's Julia, as sufficiently defined by the possessive as is Jephthah's daughter in the Old Testament tale. Jephthah's daughter—how unlike Iphigenia—does not need a name. She prefigures Mary, the handmaid of the Lord, the loving, submissive girl who will gladly die rather than cause her father to break his vow. Julia similarly needs no surname; she is simply the woman, the heroine of romantic tragedy, or, against the religious backdrop of the book, the desirable Eve who leads this Adam so deliciously and disastrously astray. The voraciously promiscuous, cunningly selfish woman we first hear about is not the Julia we see in the text. Instead we see Winston's Julia, loving and faithful, a model wife for whom her husband's love is her whole existence.

Orwell's emendations to *Paradise Lost* are as interesting as the continuities. There is an intriguing redistribution of the male-female roles. In Milton the woman falls through an inordinate desire for knowledge; she wants to know even if this means eating forbidden fruit. She is tempted by the prospect of surpassing Adam, her hierarchical superior, even by the impious dream of rivaling God. Adam, by contrast, shows no appetite for greater knowledge or higher status; he is content with things as they are, including the prohibition concerning the tree. He falls through love (the more censorious may prefer to call it uxoriousness). His wife has already fallen, is "to death devote," and he loves her too much to live without her. There can be no greater evil than separation. Even were God to supply another Eve, it would be unacceptable. And so he declares his intended defiance of God in words that make it sound as though it has already occurred:

> Some cursed fraud of enemy hath beguiled thee
> And me with thee hath ruined.[5]

That coordinating conjunction is at worst misleading, at best proleptic. Adam could still refuse the apple and negotiate with God, either resigning himself to Eve's loss or pleading for another chance, a more lenient sentence, for the culprit. It is a measure of his love for Eve that he should take it for granted that her sin and condemnation are his too:

Our state cannot be severed; we are one,
One flesh; to lose thee were to lose myself.[6]

In Orwell the situation is transposed. Winston is central in a way that Adam is not. Part One shows him locked in a lonely monologue (hence the importance of the diary for both content and form). Only with Part Two does he break through to dialogue in the idyll with Julia, and in Part Three he acquires a new partner in the iron conversations with O'Brien. Winston is the presiding consciousness, holding center stage throughout, imposing his own perspective on the action. Milton's Eve had not been so marginalized.

From the outset we see that Winston's is the role that Milton assigned to Eve. He is the intellectual rebel, desperate for knowledge (the "why" even more than the "how"), avid for forbidden fruit (the proscribed documentary evidence) that will equip him to challenge Big Brother, the otherwise omnipotent God of *Nineteen Eighty-Four*. Winston lusts for the apple. He wants not merely to know but to possess and treasure forbidden things. Once, in pure funk, he hurriedly destroyed the photograph that proved what he had long suspected—that God is a liar, the father of lies. Now he tells Julia that he would hang on to such incriminating evidence if the chance ever recurred.

The anti-intellectual Julia is scandalized by such folly. To risk life for a trifle like a photograph strikes her as lunacy. She cares nothing for documentary evidence or for the philosophical and epistemological questions that plague her lover. Who cares? is her response. Winston does: simply knowing that Big Brother is a liar is not enough; Winston is tormented by a need to prove it. His polemical, questioning mind demands that these false doctrines be branded as such. It is this same intellectual curiosity, this *libido sciendi*, that makes him hurry to the hideout, not just to meet Julia but even more to read the book. This follows upon the brutal barrage of work after the switch of enemies. He has just worked ninety hours in five days, mastering a mountain of paper but in his briefcase is still more paper that he cannot wait to devour: no rest for the thinker. The book is, of course, the ultimate apple, the most flagrantly fragrant morsel of forbidden fruit in all Oceania, and Winston, like Milton's Eve, is afire to taste it.

Julia is, like Milton's Adam, a sexual sinner, a rebel for love, untouched by any lust for knowledge. Politics bore her, and she switches off when Winston tries to discuss the meaning of Oceanic society or the philosophy of Ingsoc. She can, admittedly, be acute, outshining Winston, about the underlying import of some aspects of their society but only when they directly affect her, and so almost invariably about sexual matters. Her one perspicacious, nonsexual observation occurs when she opines that the war is a fake and that the bombs falling on London are sent by Big Brother himself. This had never occurred to Winston, for all his meditations on Oceanic society, but he at once finds it convincing, and later, in Goldstein's book, he finds Julia's intuition confirmed. But it is an intuition, a lucky strike, not the fruit of some intellectual process, some careful concatenation of thought.

Julia is in no sense intellectual. She helps to produce books but has no interest in them, regarding them as just another commodity, like jam or bootlaces. She is not a thinker. O'Brien mocks Winston for his deficiencies as a metaphysician, but Julia is not even a bad metaphysician. Where Winston thinks, she feels—hence her outburst when O'Brien posits a conflict between love and politics. Nothing for her competes with love. In this she assumes the role played by Milton's Adam. She is Winston's Julia, and in O'Brien's apartment her championship of love raises Winston to her level. Love becomes for each the best thing in the world, and the stage is set for that contest in Room 101 between the best thing and the worst.

Nevertheless Orwell highlights the difference between the two sinners, the intellectual and the sexual. Julia is delighted to be told by Winston that she is a rebel only from the waist down. For her that is the one region where it counts. What Winston intends as a reproof, however amiable, she joyfully appropriates as a compliment. She prides herself on being a sexual dissident, a vaginal insurrectionist.

All for love: that this is Julia's outlook is made clear when *the book* comes into the lovers' possession. Winston, reaching the room first, starts at once to read it. When Julia arrives, he tells her in the awed, italicized way that both he and O'Brien have of referring to it, that he has *the book*. Julia is unimpressed, pleased only that he is pleased and otherwise indifferent. She is much more interested in preparing coffee, as her prole sisters are more concerned with saucepans than with political agitation. Coffee over, she is settling down to sleep when Winston reminds her of the obligation on all members of the Brotherhood to read the book. This sister clearly find the brothers' lucubrations trivial and tedious. Eyes already closed, she tells Winston to read it aloud, explaining it as he goes: "'That's the best way'" (p. 160). The pretext is transparent. All she really wants to do is sleep. To eat, to make love, to sleep: what else is life for?

When Winston stops reading to check that she is still awake, the reply is pure Julia: "'Yes, my love, I'm listening. Go on. It's marvellous'" (p. 161). The conciliatory lie, the term of endearment, the bogus encouragement, the refusal to hurt his feelings or puncture his enthusiasm—Julia has all she wants, but if Winston needs something extra, she will not grudge it him. We never know at what point she falls asleep; we do know that the book cannot persuade her to stay awake and that boredom, even more than fatigue, causes her to drop off. She simply does not care about the things that obsess Winston, but that proves that she loves him, not his politics or philosophy.

That is why it rings false when, just before the arrest, Julia uncharacteristically repeats her lover's lugubrious words: "'We are the dead,' echoed Julia dutifully" (p. 174). Why? Nothing in the text prepares us for such morbidness from her. She is the optimist, heedless, living for the moment (coffee, sex, sleep), refusing to speculate on the dark future, trusting to her penchant for eluding trouble, her gift for staying alive. She is a strange melange of qualities: incurious, shortsighted, almost prole-like in her distaste for general ideas, with no intellectual concern for the society she lives in, merely a cunning animal resolve to evade its restrictions. Yet she is practical and organized; she initiates and manages the love affair, plots their love trysts with maximum efficiency, and knows how to get hold of the best chocolate, coffee, sugar, and other commodities. She is good with her hands, and it is she who plans to plaster up the rat hole.

for nothing lovelier can be found
In woman than to study household good.[7]

Julia passes the Miltonic test with flying colors. Yet this practical competence accompanies a kind of dottiness, a scatterbrained quality, reflected in her response to Winston's surprise at her acquisition of real tea: "'There's been a lot of tea about lately. They've captured India, or something' she said vaguely" (p. 115).

What we never catch her speaking is the language of despair. The pessimistic Winston, so ready to meet trouble halfway, declares them to be the dead—a judgment repeated by O'Brien when he deludes them about the Brotherhood—but Julia cannot abide such masculine morbidity. "'We're not dead yet,' said Julia prosaically." When Winston retorts that it is only a matter of time—six months, a year—that his words are essentially, if not literally, true, she erupts and irritably rebukes him: "'Oh, rubbish! Which would you sooner sleep with, me or a skeleton? Don't you enjoy being alive? . . . Don't you like *this?*'" (p. 111). *This* is the female form she is pressing against him. If he likes it, as he surely does, he should forget all the nonsense about dying and enjoy what is his.

So why does Julia turn recreant to her own breezy *carpe diem* outlook to echo Winston's gloomy presentiments? Certainly Orwell wants the dramatic effect of the double repetition. Julia repeats Winston's words, and then the iron voice from behind the picture confirms the assertion, changing only the personal pronoun: *we* becomes *you*, as the devils occupy Eden (p. 174). The dramatic effect is electric, but it is achieved at the cost of Julia's psychological consistency. Why is she suddenly spouting her husband's pessimism? She still is not a skeleton and has no reason to forsake her optimistic belief that she can stay one step ahead of the Thought Police. Why is she now concurring with what she had always derided?

Part Three is a return to the isolated, womanless man. Julia vanishes, carried out like a sack of potatoes, not to reappear until the appalling coda. In the one explicit reference to her, O'Brien describes her conversion as "perfect," all the "dirty-mindedness" burned out of her (p. 205). How she is broken we never know; that she is is depressingly clear. Winston is now the focus of attention. He continues to love Julia, but O'Brien's blueprint for human nature is ominous: all elemental human relationships, parents and children, husbands and wives, are to be phased out: "In future there will be no wives and no friends. . . . There will be no love, except the love of Big Brother" (p. 212). Winston regards these claims as wildly extravagant; even in the pit of humiliation, weeping and debased, he still proclaims his defiance: "'I have not betrayed Julia'"—and O'Brien is forced to agree (p. 217).

O'Brien is too honest to claim victories before they are won. The cry of devotion that breaks from Winston in his dream proves that he still loves Julia: "It was as though she had got into the texture of his skin. In that moment he had loved her far more than he had ever done when they were together and free" (p. 222). It is a striking tribute to the endurance of a man whom certain critics too pharisaically dismiss as a weakling. Despite the torture and brainwashing, Winston loves Julia more than ever. Big Brother, the monopolist of love, is understandably outraged and schemes how to drive the interloper from Winston's heart so that he can take exclusive possession.

His success, the totality of the rout suffered by human love, is what is so dispiriting about this text. The great affair ends in disinterest and fitful dislike. The inseparable, devoted lovers betray each other. O'Brien had ironically congratulated them for being so frank: "'You did well to tell me. . . . It is necessary for us to know everything'" (p. 140). Naturally. Satan, eavesdropping in Eden, learns about the forbidden tree and now knows how to go about ruining the lovers:

> Yet let me not forget what I have gained
> From their own mouths.[8]

O'Brien also knows, from Winston's own mouth, what he most prizes and fears, and the brilliantly effective use to which O'Brien puts this knowledge in Room 101 is proved in the shamefully different cry uttered by Winston—"'Do it to Julia! Not me!'" (p. 227)—so nau-seatingly opposite to the cry of love in the prison cell. "'You will do what is required of you'" (p. 226). O'Brien's disparaging prognosis is fully vin-dicated: the devoted lover cracks when tested. Burke calls conduct the only language that rarely lies.[9] Winston's conduct in Room 101 revokes forever his right to say that he has not betrayed Julia.

We despise what we betray. Winston betrays Julia and himself. In the final chapter Julia is nameless, has become simply 'she.' Signifi-cantly Winston is also unable to name the rats "even in his thoughts," though their smell is forever in his nostrils. Julia and the rats are henceforth nameless; it is thus that Winston hopes they will cease to haunt him. "He had seen her; he had even spoken to her. There was no danger in it" (p. 230). The danger is not from the Thought Police, for they no longer interest themselves in his doings, but from Julia herself. Winston is cured of love. The passion that brought him to Room 101 is extinguished forever.

"He could have arranged to meet her a second time if either of them had wanted to" (pp. 230–31). If there is hope, it is in the proles. These are two empty ifs, two contrary-to-fact conditionals. They do not want to meet again. They do not want to meet at all. They do so accidentally in a chillingly lifeless encounter. He follows her un-eagerly; she apathetically tries to shake him off and then just as drear-ily resigns herself to his company. All vitality has hemorrhaged away; we watch wraiths, not people. He encircles her waist in dull routine, and she just as listlessly submits. Here, in these burned-out people, we remember *The Waste Land*, the little life, the dried tubers. April, Eliot's cruelest month, is the month when Winston's story opens. Now it is March again, a "vile, biting day," the earth "like iron," the grass "dead," the only flowers "a few crocuses . . . dismembered by the wind"—fit setting for the zombies who were once Romeo and Juliet.

There is no one to stop them making love; they might just as easily attempt levitation. The mere thought that there is no external check to lying down togther to do "that" causes Winston's flesh to freeze with horror. The best-trained dogs, as Orwell says, are those that obey without a whip (*CEJL*, 3:212). Julia, once so quick and lively—she "hops" over the fallen tree to part the bushes at their first love tryst—has become ponderous and unresponsive, sister to the typist of *The Waste Land*. Winston, however, unlike her young man carbuncular, is not prepared to make a welcome of indifference; the very idea of sex revolts him. He is conscious of the surprising, repugnant thickness of her waist ("the sweet supple waist" that once invited embrace); her body is corpselike, stone rather than flesh. In Eliot's poem the woman suffers sex like an enema; in Orwell's novel both partners are totally disenchanted, following the Strephon of Swift's scatological poems into a state of morbid alienation from life itself.[10]

Winston makes no attempt to kiss or even speak to her. He catches her looking at him with contempt and wonders whether to attribute this to past events or to his present repulsive appearance. There has been a physical deterioration; the maltreatment in Miniluv and the readdiction to gin have had their effect. Julia too has coarsened, becoming ponderously unattractive. But the damage within, the spiritual lesions, are far more horrific than anything done to their bodies. Disliking themselves, they dislike each other. How can Winston love a woman whom he wanted to give to the rats? How can he respect himself after devising such an escape?

Feelings are all that matter, the lovers had agreed in happier times when they discussed their eventual capture. They concluded that what is done is unimportant since deeds are secondary to feelings: "'What you say or do doesn't matter; only feelings matter. If they could make me stop loving you—that would be the real betrayal'" (p. 135). Julia reassures Winston; even Big Brother cannot do that. Unfortunately the severance between acts and feelings, being and consciousness, is not so clear-cut as the lovers optimistically assume; mind and matter, however mysteriously, modify each other. After Room 101 Winston discovers that he cannot love Julia; he cannot keep his actions in one sealed compartment and his unaffected feelings in another. There is no human nature apart from deeds; we cannot live divorced from our actions. We are the deed's creatures, and our feelings must be affected by our behavior: "'After that, you don't feel the same towards the other person any longer,'" says Julia, and Winston knows only too well how true this is (p. 232).

The erstwhile lovers have no more to say to each other apart from the transparent lie about meeting again. *Lie* is in fact too harsh a term for something so vague and so patently intended not to deceive. They are used up, irresolute, volitionless. Winston makes a halfhearted attempt to follow her before the memory of the warm café and the ever-flowing gin comes between him and the desultory chase. He could still catch up but is instead relieved to lose sight of her in the crowd. The flat, lifeless quality of the writing once again recalls Eliot, especially *The Hollow Men*:

> This is the way the world ends
> Not with a bang but a whimper.[11]

There could be no more apt description of how the passion of Winston and Julia peters out to its sad conclusion.

We are nevertheless justified in describing *Nineteen Eighty-Four* as a great love story, even if it appalls rather than inspires, for the failure of the affair with Julia leads to the consummation of the competing passion. Big Brother is present from the first, a face on a poster, ruggedly handsome, tantalizing the hero. Periodically he takes from his pocket a coin with this face and interrogates it to pierce the mystery of the smile hidden beneath the moustache. Against the unmistakable religious background of Winston's rebellion, the coin recalls Jesus with the coin of the tribute, sidestepping his enemies' malice with the distinction between the things that are Caesar's and the things that are God's. It is, alas, a distinction no longer relevant in Oceania; the new Caesar demands everything and, by the infamous climax, has got it. Winston has at last deciphered the smile; he loves Big Brother. We leave the two characters who opened the novel, estranged and distrustful, now joined in beatific bliss, at one in a dream of love that will end only when the wished-for bullet shatters Winston's skull: though he slay me, yet will I trust in him.

Here is a crescendo of devotion to balance the diminuendo of the sexual debacle, a triumph of love, however much we deplore it. This love is the first of the many varieties that the book presents. Winston sees all four government buildings from his window, but there is no doubt which is the most significant: "The Ministry of Love was the really frightening one. There were no windows in it at all" (p. 7). For no immediately assignable reason, this second sentence provokes a tremor of fear. Love is, after all, *the* private activity, degraded when it becomes a public performance; Cordelia is a heroine for refusing to go public with her most intimate feelings. Isn't it fitting that a structure dedicated to love should be without windows? Those within, wrapped up in each other, have no cause to look out, while those outside have no business to look in. Only satiated lovers and voyeurs require windows.

Yet even before we hear about the barbed wire entanglements, the machine-gun nests, and the gorilla-like guards roaming the surrounding streets, we sense something sinister in the mere mention of the windowless building and wonder apprehensively what is going on behind those blank walls. It is "a place impossible to enter except on official business" (p. 7)—exactly what the vagina itself has become in Oceania. "Official business" is exactly what that dismal, functional weekly routine between Winston and his wife, Katherine, amounts to. Indoctrinated to abhor the sexual act, Katherine nevertheless insists that her husband should enter her upon the official business of making a child for the Party. Love has been debased to a productive process, a still regrettably necessary component in the manufacture of a certain commodity. The building that is the official residence of love in Oceania should alert us for the hideous distortions to come.

Winston comes to Miniluv through his involvement in two love affairs, and, significantly, the rival lovers appear simultaneously and together. He is about to take his seat for the Hate, that Oceanic Angelus, when O'Brien and Julia unexpectedly enter to complete the triangle that every love story demands. Winston's distrust of the girl contrasts with his deep attraction to the man. So unlike the little, beetle-like intellectuals whom Winston regards as typical of Ingsoc, O'Brien has the same macho appeal as Big Brother—appropriately, since he turns out to be a kind of proxy lover, a deputy wooer. He is large, burly, strong, with a prizefighter's physique, yet also, remarkably, possessing grace, intelligence, and "a certain charm of manner"

(p. 12). So determined is Orwell to convey this striking fusion of qualities that he violates his own narrative mode in order to do so. O'Brien has a trick of resettling his spectacles on his nose that is curiously civilized: "It was a gesture which, if anyone had still thought in such terms, might have recalled an eighteenth-century nobleman offering his snuffbox" (p. 12). Clearly no one is any longer thinking in such terms; Orwell gatecrashes his own fiction to supply the image that would otherwise be lost.

Such is the rival wooer sent by Big Brother to counter the sexual blandishments of the woman, and, given the kind of man that Winston is, we must pronounce it an excellent choice. Winston is bowled over by an irresistible blend of unorthodoxy, strength, and intelligence. It is, as we have already seen, entirely plausible that the frail, self-doubting Winston should fall for this robust figure, just as it is undeniable that there is something wrong from the start in the attraction. Winston's thoughts are initially about O'Brien rather than Julia. His dream before the book begins is of O'Brien, and traditionally the lover dreams of the loved one. It is O'Brien's voice that promises a meeting in the place of no darkness, and despite Winston's assertion that "you did not have friends nowadays, you had comrades," he is nevertheless convinced, without ever having exchanged words, that O'Brien is his intimate friend.

Throughout Part One, whenever Winston is tempted to despair, O'Brien's face inspires him, and his wilting courage stiffens of its own accord. We need not turn so common a cliché into a conscious phallic metaphor, but clearly the mere thought of O'Brien fortifies Winston, much as Adam declares that, with Eve looking on, he will give the devil a harder fight.[12] Winston is similarly uplifted by a vision of O'Brien's face and by the thought that the diary is dedicated to him. With O'Brien in mind, he commits to its pages the irreducible epistemological defiance that two plus two equals four. His rebellion is shaped by O'Brien at every stage of its progress. He ends Part One invoking the talismanic face against the despondency that follows the shock encounter with Julia. That he fails—O'Brien's face merges ominously with the tyrant's, recapitulating that similar fusion at the end of *Animal Farm*—does not alter the fact that in his trouble he turns instinctively to O'Brien for support.

Even after the discovery of Julia, he continues to be drawn irresistibly to O'Brien. When he tells Julia of his wild impulse to contact O'Brien, she, far from disapproving, thinks it perfectly natural to trust someone on no more than a flash of the eye. When O'Brien finally takes the initiative, Winston's excitement is palpable on the page. The parallelism of the two affairs is reinforced by O'Brien's irony in choosing to accost Winston at the spot where Julia made her overture. Aware of "someone larger than himself" behind him, Winston turns to confront the man in his life. The long-awaited rendezvous is rendered in a style suspiciously close to that of popular romantic fiction, with the fluttering heroine and the masterful hero of her dreams: "At last they were face to face, and it seemed that his only impulse was to run away. His heart bounded violently. He would have been incapable of speaking" (p. 128). Change personal pronoun and possessives, and the idiom is that of women's magazines, redolent of dreamy lovers rather than political conspirators, a starstruck girl meeting Robert Redford rather than a malcontent being conscripted for terrorism. O'Brien assumes the stereotypical male role, taking his slighter companion's arm, leading him as they stroll side by side down the corridor, directing the conversation, arranging the assignation.

Winston is still an admirer in O'Brien's apartment, though his hero's role has changed. Since Julia, Winston's sexual partner, is with him, O'Brien appears in another guise, that of the Promethean rebel, the priest of the brotherhood. (O'Brien, as Big Brother's deputy, represents a love hostile to Julia's but annexing the sexual with every other type of affection in its totalitarian voracity.) The elegant apartment, the altar-desk with its mass of duties, the initiatory catechism, the strange, impassive acolyte who serves the priest, the communion service with its wine and host, the formidable celebrant: all of this ritual, according so well with O'Brien's Catholic name, is at once impressive and intimidating. The new catechumens, so unused to luxury and privacy—the telescreen is amazingly turned off—are nervous, uneasy, but above all awestruck. O'Brien is so clearly a man of power;

even if they do not live to see it in person, they know they have joined the winning side.

Remarkably Winston's admiration, even affection, survives the disclosure that the underground hero is really the high priest of Oceania. Before this revelation, in the windowless, electric-lit cell, he is confirmed in O'Brien's wisdom, for this truly is the place with no darkness. He is honest enough to admit that he will not use the razor when it arrives, but the fact that he expects it reveals his unshakable trust in O'Brien's word. Winston's mistake when O'Brien enters is pardonable because it is the promised meeting and because it seems part of a regular sequence. O'Brien ostensibly enters as the third member of a series of thought criminals: Ampleforth, Parsons, and himself. Parsons is a real stunner—"'*You* here!'" (p. 184)—but O'Brien is a bombshell as Winston learns that he is facing the chief Thought Policeman. Yet strangely there is no reproach at betrayal. Indeed when O'Brien preemptively declares that Winston had always known the truth, Winston unprotestingly assents. Perhaps he is thinking of that inveterate human tendency to invest in welcome delusion, to believe what it comforts us to believe: he had so wanted O'Brien to be Prometheus, and the result is a rebel of the imagination, every bit as fictitious as Comrade Ogilvy.

Certainly a Winston raging at betrayal would have been harder pressed to sustain admiration for the traitor or go on harboring that sense of intimate intensity with O'Brien that he had always experienced. The relationship is strangely personal, peculiarly close, affectionate, even devoted. For Winston, O'Brien is both tormentor and protector, inquisitor and friend. O'Brien, in turn, has a genuine solicitude for his prisoner: "'You are in my keeping. For seven years I have watched over you. . . . I shall save you, I shall make you perfect'" (p. 193). If this were hypocrisy, it would be less frightening; however grudgingly, we are forced to call this love, albeit a type we prefer not to exist. Winston remarks for the first time the fatigued, aging face of his savior, and this reinforces the hint of a careworn father, grieved at his son's straying and obliged, for the culprit's own good, to chastise him. The reprimanding voice is that of a doctor, a teacher, a priest— all of them the caring professions, persuaders rather than punishers.

O'Brien invariably calls Winston by his Christian name and plainly regards him as a prize, worth all the trouble expended upon him: a wayward but promising child, a star pupil if only he bucks up his ideas. Like many another devoted dominie, O'Brien loses his temper when the pupil is lazy or obdurate, but if he inflicts pain, he also brings succour. Winston finds himself "sitting up with O'Brien's arm round his shoulder" (p. 198). It is the quintessential human gesture, linking O'Brien with Winston's mother and the lifeboat-woman. Winston, reciprocating, clings like a child to this protector who will shield him from the pain emanating inexplicably from some unknown source. Solicitous sadist and grateful victim: we are surely in strange psychological territory in *Nineteen Eighty-Four*.

O'Brien "gently" rebukes Winston for being a slow learner, and the offender "blubbers" his defensive apology. After each bout of agony he turns in loving gratitude to the inquisitor: "At sight of the heavy, lined face . . . his heart seemed to turn over. If he could have moved he would have stretched out a hand and laid it on O'Brien's arm. He had never loved him so deeply as at this moment, and not merely because he had stopped the pain" (p. 200). This is one of the most remarkable passages in all prison literature. Only the fact that he is strapped down prevents the victim from fondling his torturer. Soon Winston will cower in fear of this zealot who will assuredly vaporize him, but for the moment "it made no difference . . . they were intimates." The torturer strikingly shares the sentiment. In *Paradise Lost* the self-disparaging Eve deplores the fact that the relationship with Adam is so tilted in her favor:

> I chiefly who enjoy
> So far the happier lot, enjoying thee
> Pre-eminent by so much odds, while thou
> Like consort to thyself canst nowhere find.[13]

Winston, as we have seen, finds it easier to make love than conversation with Julia; the irony is that the only like consort he can find is O'Brien, who tortures him. Yet to talk and, more important still, to be understood is a relief, even when it can only happen in the cellars of Miniluv.

To be understood involves a kind of intellectual intercourse, a congress of minds, a spiritual mating. O'Brien recognizes the affinity as much as Winston, endorsing, "with a smile," Winston's diary comment that they relate to each other in a sense transcending mere friendship or enmity. They are intellectual *inamoratos*: "'Your mind appeals to me. It resembles my own mind except that you happen to be insane'" (p. 205). Julia has the sex appeal, but O'Brien is the intellectual and the conceptual charmer.

Winston is especially moved when O'Brien generously concedes the claim not to have betrayed Julia. It is the sheer intelligence, the unfailing ability to understand without the need for explanation, that so entrances Winston. He is so busy being grateful that he fails to see how "thoughtfully" O'Brien is looking at him; the adverb might have worried a man not so emotionally overcome. He is still awash with sentiment as he dreams in his cell of a sojourn in the Golden Country in the company of his loved ones: his mother, Julia, and, remarkably, O'Brien. What is O'Brien doing in such a setting and in such a company? Winston dreams of "merely sitting in the sun, talking of peaceful things" (p. 218). With O'Brien? With the priest of power, fresh from his frenzied paean in praise of mayhem? How is the boot in the face to figure in such tranquil conversation? These incongruities serve merely to highlight the hold that, despite everything, O'Brien continues to have upon Winston's heart.

The puzzle is why Winston should abominate Big Brother while revering, even loving, his henchman. Why is the god odious and his priest admirable? The inconsistency is eliminated in the book's conclusion when Winston's hatred of Big Brother is changed to love. Just before sending Winston to Room 101, O'Brien reproaches him for his intended infidelity—"'you had thoughts of deceiving me'"—and, like a sorrowful husband with an errant wife, he takes the transgressor's shoulders "between his strong hands" (p. 224). The post–Room 101 Winston recalls O'Brien's assurance that "'what happens to you here is for ever'" (p. 203). It is the language of passionate commitment that lovers habitually use to each other. This is the last mention of O'Brien in the text (significantly, Winston can still name him as he cannot name Julia, further confirmation of the love that prevails), and we take leave of O'Brien speaking "a true word." The book vindicates O'Brien as truth-teller, for all is as he foretold: Winston and Big Brother, the erstwhile enemies, are now blissfully united.

The secret of the smile beneath the moustache is finally revealed. It is that of a god secure in his omnipotence, of a world in which religion and politics are one, with no space between them. The ancient distinction between Caesar and God is cancelled; Caesar is God, the one true god who will brook no competing affection and no rival loyalty. Big Brother may well smile in view of his defeat of the rival gods who challenge him in the book: the god of traditional religion that Winston rejects as a myth and the god he claims to represent, the spirit of man that will, so he insists, finally thwart Big Brother.

Everything slots into place once we recognize that Oceania is a theocracy, Big Brother a god, Ingsoc a religion. The power of this new religion is exhibited in the ritual of the Hate, hellfire sermon and *auto-da-fé* combined, the woman responding to her telescreen savior, like Saint Teresa to Christ, while Winston hides from the other face of God—Jehovah, ineluctable avenger. His evasion is as futile as that of the traditional sinner; the Thought Police will get him whether he writes or destroys the diary: God is not mocked. What the old religions aspired to, the new one has achieved. Big Brother is infallible to a degree undreamed of by the most fervid of ultramontanes. He can annihilate and create too, as Comrad Ogilvy demonstrates when called into existence as miraculously as Adam, hagiographic equivalent of the legendary saints, an example of total dedication, a eunuch for Oceania's sake. Julia, by contrast, is a sexual heretic, rebel from the waist down, with sex for its own sake the extent of her particular *non serviam*. Winston is also a sex criminal, but his root offense is *ownlife*, the heresy of individualism. Both lovers are like the obsessed sinners of traditional religion, feverishly digging their own pits. Every sinner confesses, as Julia says, but confession, as O'Brien insists, is as good for the soul in the new religion as Catholic apologists have claimed it to be in the old.

The new god spurns loveless obedience as inefficacious unto

salvation. The function of Room 101 in Oceanic theology is to eradicate every possible competing passion: thou shalt love thy God with thy whole heart and thy whole mind, no corner, however minute, reserved for lesser loyalties. In Room 101 one learns to value God above all else, to devote one's life *ad maiorem gloriam dei*. Winston, loving Julia as Milton's Adam loves Eve, wilfully rejects creator for creature, and the sinner must be taught to detest his choice, for what good is a forced obedience? Satan could have been barred from Eden, Winston arrested the moment he bought the diary, but to what purpose? How is the sinner to be redeemed unless first permitted to sin? Charrington's shop, like the tree in Eden, is placed in the sinner's path, and he falls that he may be cleansed.

Mere outward conformity is a scandal to the puritans who control Oceania. One must love God because he chastises. Miscasting himself as Prometheus, Winston must be schooled to his proper role as Job. *Areopagitica* is obscenely parodied in the argument that good only comes via evil;[14] the moment of explusion from Eden is as terrifying as that moment when Winston hears the iron voice from behind the picture, but no more for Winston than for Adam is paradise irretrievably lost. O'Brien, playing Michael to Winston's Adam, describes the three stages in the sinner's regeneration—learning, understanding, accceptance—and warns that the first two are necessarily painful. But the pain is purgatorial, God being cruel to be kind.

The new God declines to lose a single soul, like Origen's deity rather than the more orthodox figure of the Last Judgment. Hell has no place in Oceanic theology, for hell is God's shame, his admission that there are wills too stubborn, evils too obdurate, even for his love to overcome; every hellbound soul is the devil's victory. The devils of Oceania win no victories, are permitted only to exist to demonstrate the futile folly of seduction and to exalt God the more by this exhibition of impotence. Winston hears O'Brien's consoling voice assuring him that he is at last in the hands of the omniscient, infallible healer; O'Brien refers to Julia's perfect conversion as a textbook case—redundantly since there is no other kind in Oceania: "'everyone is washed clean'" (p. 202). No one is lost in this monstrous parody of Christian salvation.

The new religion's power is shown in various ways. Winston thinks it is quite possible that the drunken prole harridan may well be the silent, dignified lady who was his mother so long ago: "It was possible that people changed somewhat after twenty years in a forced labour-camp" (p. 181). It recalls Swift's flayed woman whose appearance was changed for the worse, and the calculated understatement with its disciplined bitterness, its deadpan intensity, reveals the Swift in Orwell.[15] With God all things are possible; perhaps the foul-mouthed, vomiting prole was once the grave, stately lady. Not the heavens but the cellars of Miniluv declare the glory of the new God.

But it is in its disciples' fanaticism that the power of the new creed is most impressively displayed. O'Brien is transfigured as he chants his paean to power. Winston cowers before the enormous face, "filled with a sort of exaltation, a lunatic intensity," the face of the mystic as seen by the bewildered, fearful outsider (p. 201). The new religion repudiates the whole Christian-humanist ethos: "'Above all, we do not allow the dead to rise up against us,'" and the vetoed resurrection makes unpersons of Christ, Shakespeare, and all the other champions of man's allegedly unconquerable spirit (p. 202). Humanism is as dead as the Galilean. As we shall see in the next chapter, the peculiar scandal of Orwell's work is its implication that these two bereavements are related; there is a shocking correlation between political, moral, and religious decline (*CEJL*, 2:33, 3:123, 126, 127, 4:117).

Even as O'Brien rhapsodizes, Winston is struck by the speaker's aging face, impotence in its most absolute form of death visibly overcoming the power worshipper. But by allowing O'Brien an insight into the discrepancy between his words and his state, Orwell deliberately renounces a golden opportunity for ironically subverting the rhetoric. O'Brien, as always reading Winston's mind, dismisses his own approaching dissolution as trifling when set against the immortality of his adored collective. Who cares about personal extinction when "'the weariness of the cell is the vigour of the organism'" (p. 209)? Winston, by contrast, collapses when forced to confront his own physical ruin; his god fails where O'Brien's triumphs.

We are on the fringe here of what Orwell referred to as the major problem of our time: the tragedy of finitude following upon the decline of belief in personal immortality. Throughout the text Winston anguishes over the certainty of annihilation—not merely of being tortured to death but, in the phrase that he and O'Brien both use, of being lifted clean out of the stream of history. Death is an obsession in the book—not simply the violence of vaporization but death as the natural, unavoidable terminus toward which all life is moving. "'Alone—free—the human being is . . . doomed to die, which is the greatest of all failures'" (pp. 209–10). The problem at root is that of our lost immortality and how we propose to solve it in the religious wasteland of our time. O'Brien tackles and "solves" this problem by denying the value of individual life; the individual is merely a cell, insignificant and expendable. All that matters is the survival of the beloved collective. However repugnant to Christian-humanist principles, O'Brien's solution works, enabling him to discount his death and to give a sense of purpose to his brief existence. He disparages individual death because he despises individual life; neither matters. Only Big Brother does, and he is immortal. Ingsoc's claim to be a religion is nowhere better vindicated than in its willingness to confront the problem that every religion has always attempted to solve.

No one can fail to see how extensively Orwell has plundered the doctrines of the old religion to expose the iniquities of the new. So many of the tenets of Oceania are akin to key Christian beliefs: that God must be loved as well as obeyed; that sin is essentially an affair of the heart, a will to rebel rather than the act itself; that the real offense is the impious thought even when it does not issue in action; that sinners must be permitted to go their deviant way so that the joy in heaven will be the greater at their eventual contrite return; that nothing, finally, is more important than to die as the friend of God. The hideous fascination of *Nineteen Eighty-Four* springs from the teasing tangle of correspondences that Orwell weaves between Christianity and Ingsoc. But even more important than the parallels are the contrasts, the shocking discrepancies that surface just when the similarities seem most pronounced. Ingsoc is at once so like, yet perversely unlike, the creed that it wickedly apes; the effect is like looking into a mirror to see a grimacing simian mask.

In tiny detail as in sustained analogy, Orwell forges the links between the two faiths. The language used to describe Goldstein comes not from politics but from demonology: "the primal traitor, the earliest defiler of the Party's purity" (p. 13). He is the arch heresiarch; he wanders the world diabolically seeking the ruin of souls, and, devil-like, will do so for all time. The first denunciation of Winston as sinner comes, significantly, from a nine-year-old boy: out of the mouths of babes. Both Winston and O'Brien refer to the dream of seven years ago; the number, far from being arbitrary, is the biblical number signifying salvation and success, figuring in Joseph's inspired exegesis of Pharaoh's dream, as also in Jacob's marriage exertions. The religious allusions are abundant and obvious: the coin of Big Brother and the coin of Caesar with which his enemies tried to trap Jesus; the hagiographic inspiration of Comrade Ogilvy; the six-day creation of the new political world at Hate Week, challenging God's labor of love in Genesis; the recurring references to death as man's single greatest challenge—all place the book within an unmistakably religious context. When Syme defines orthodoxy as not thinking, when Winston concludes that the Party commands a rejection of all empirical evidence in favor of faith, they are echoing Feuerbach's attack on traditional religion: "he who appeals to experience renounces faith."[16] At a crucial point in their debate, O'Brien directly asks, "'Do you believe in God, Winston?'" (p. 214)—a question crucial to the outcome of the contest between sadist and victim. We cannot fully understand what is happening in *Nineteen Eighty-Four* unless we recognize the importance of its religious dimension.

For a militant atheist like Orwell to attack religion is scarcely surprising; what is surprising is the nature of the religion attacked. The rulers of Oceania detest the traditional God of established religion. Theirs is a new, savage God whose origin Orwell unexpectedly locates in the age of unbelief. He goes scandalously further in suggesting that it required such an age to spawn such an idol. It is a stunning conclusion to Orwell's work—at once the predictable culmination of his antireligious views and yet remarkably not an attack on religion at all but on atheistic totalitarianism, the most savagely intolerant creed ever known. No longer, as in progressive leftist wisdom, is God the enemy of man, religion the foe of humanism; the enemy is now revealed as man himself, especially, as the orthodox had always insisted, the man who usurpingly makes himself a god.

The relevance of *Nineteen Eighty-Four* to our time stems from Orwell's insight that the threat today comes from the new atheistic religions that have hatched among the ruins of institutional Christianity. There are no traditional believers in *Nineteen Eighty-Four,* simply a good and a bad atheist, and the text enacts the struggle between their respective creeds: humanism, the religion of the past with Winston as its last, doomed advocate, and totalitarian sadism, the religion of the present and, the book's pessimism insists, of the future, with O'Brien as its triumphant high priest. The bad atheist wins, climactic scandal in a thoroughly scandalous work.

Walking through London, Winston comes upon certain buildings, once churches, now "put to other uses" (p. 81). From a conventional, "progressive" perspective this sounds, initially at least, like improvement. In fact the erstwhile churches have been converted into war museums and torture chambers in an expropriation as calamitous as that of Mr. Jones in *Animal Farm.* We inevitably protest that it need not be so; religion can disappear without something far worse succeeding it. Powerful voices from the past will disagree. *Entweder Gott oder Abgott* ("either God or idol") insists Luther, and Dostoyevsky tells us that everyone must finally choose between Christ and the Grand Inquisitor. What is undeniable is that Orwell, for whatever reason, shows traditional religion replaced by an infinitely worse creed, with all of the defects of historical Christianity monstrously magnified and none of the merits remaining. His text gives no comfort to those who assume that atheism must embody a higher stage of civilization than Christianity or that the waning of traditional belief is a matter for unqualified celebration; it might almost be cited as proof of Luther's fearful option, with Big Brother as terrifying an idol today as Baal or Moloch in former ages. Dostoyevsky too would have recognized in Orwell's text the age-old struggle between freedom and slavery and would have found within its pages the terminus toward which *The Devils* pointed.

Luther and Dostoyevsky are, admittedly, strange territory for a man of Orwell's beliefs and background. Surely, it will be objected, this is not at all the context in which to begin to assess him. Yet Kolakowski tells us that we still carry within us the unanswered questions that have troubled theologians over the centuries; we simply phrase them differently.[16] Beneath their modern garb, these ancient dilemmas still hold us in thrall, so that, for example, the problem of nature and grace goes on perplexing us under its new name of determinism and responsibility. Winston's predicament in Room 101 is a modern rendition of that ancient quarrel, with despair flowing from the bitter admission that there is no grace, only a nature irredeemably fallen. Politics in our time has become a pursuit of the old religious questions in new guise.[17] What makes Orwell so urgent an interpreter of contemporary history is his intuition that twentieth-century politics has increasingly become disguised soteriology, the pursuit of religion by other means. The key to our century, not least to its horrors, is to study what happens in practice when this substitution occurs, and no one is better qualified to act as tutor than Orwell. His relentless inquiry into modern political iniquity led him inevitably to analyze the animal responsible, and if he is to the twentieth what Hobbes was to the seventeenth century, it is because for both the political analysis is finally grounded upon certain revelations of man.[18] *Nineteen Eighty-Four* is Orwell's climactic political nightmare, manifesting the diabolism that the orthodox legend, from Marlowe to Dostoyevsky, has always shown as the dire terminus of the attempt to coerce the earth into becoming heaven.

This is why, despite the many correspondences, it is where Orwell diverges from Milton that his text speaks most pointedly to our own condition. For Milton God is not the enemy but the loving, forgiving father; the enemy is Satan, "the tempter ere th' accuser of mankind," foe to God and man alike.[19] Milton's is a three-dimensional universe, with man the prize in a contest between heaven and hell. Orwell as atheist excludes heaven from his scheme of things and conflates God and Satan in one malign, omnipotent figure. O'Brien is both tempter and accuser, the serpent of this tale, yet also, shockingly, God's fanatic, in God's employ. Orwell's universe contains only man and man's adversary, a Satan without any power in heaven or earth to tame his malice. In Orwell the two sinners go together to O'Brien, believing him to be an ally against the tyrant. There can be no equivalent situation in Milton because his God is man's ally, whereas Orwell's is the fiend and O'Brien his agent for ensnaring man. On his own testimony, Milton's Satan has nothing against the human pair; he ruins them in retaliation against God. O'Brien, by contrast, destroys the lovers because his God commands it. God (it is what atheistic progressives had always taught) is the enemy of man. In *Nineteen Eighty-Four* it is still so, but the hostile God is now atheistic and progressive, as startling a switch of alliances as any occurring in Oceania. Traditional foes and traditional friends have unnervingly changed places.

Ampleforth's vaporization makes this plain. His offense is to let the word *God* remain as a word in a poem. His defense, based on the linguistic difficulty of finding an alternative, is disregarded. Big Brother is a jealous God who cannot abide the mere mention of his predecessor. He has appropriated that predecessor's injunction for his own cult: thou shalt not have strange gods before me. In Oceania everything is topsy-turvy. Ampleforth has violated the prime commandment; how can he be allowed to live? By contrast Big Brother's disdain for the proles touches bottom in his readiness to let them worship the old God in the old way if they so wish. Ampleforth must die for letting a mere word (not even his own) stand, whereas the proles may restore Christianity itself because nothing they do matters.

The universe of *Paradise Lost* remains to the end irreducibly threefold: heaven, hell, earth. The world of *Nineteen Eighty-Four* is depressingly single, with heaven and earth subsumed into hell. The unconverted Winston could rightfully echo Marlowe's Faustus: "Why, this is hell, nor am I out of it."[20] What seemed a recapitulation of Origen is really an antithesis: in Origen everyone is saved, but in Oceania everyone is lost.

6

THE DARKER SELF

How could one fail to detect the influence of *Gulliver's Travels* on *Nineteen Eighty-Four*? It is so massively present, in part and in whole, in individual incident and in overall structure, in detail and in ground plan. The *Travels* have a paradigmatic import for the later book, providing a kind of template, a grid for plotting the parallel course of Winston's experience. We easily trace the shaping force of Gulliver's several voyages on different facets of Winston's development. Important elements of Swift's art—Brobdingnag, the Struldbruggs, the Yahoos, the Academy of Lagado and the island of sorcerers, Gulliver's indoctrination by the horses and his final horrified rejection of sex with his "Yahoo" wife—leave their indelible imprint upon events in Oceania. The problem is not to find correspondences but to restrict them to manageable proportions.

Our introduction to the strange new society—which might so chillingly become our own—with its telescreens and Thought Police, its Two Minutes Hate and memory holes, its Newspeak and double-think, its Spies and its Anti-Sex League, is structurally similar to a Gulliverian journey into remote parts. (In Swift, too, what at first seems totally alien turns out to be mortifyingly familiar.) True, Swift always begins in normalcy. Gulliver is at home in England with his family before being dispatched to his new adventure. Orwell, by contrast, opens with a clock striking thirteen, alerting us at once to a situation both ominous and novel. By the end of Chapter One a mass of information has been communicated about the new society. Orwell spoke of writing "a novel about the future . . . a fantasy, but in the form of a naturalistic novel," though we must not misinterpret fantasy as meaning delusion (*CEJL*, 4:378). If the fantasy is to work as a cautionary tale, it must be rooted in truth, and in 1950 E. M. Forster shrewdly declared that "there is not a monster in that hateful apocalypse which does not exist in embryo today."[1] The land is Airstrip One, but its capital is London; the currency is dollars, but the pub proles are unmistakably English. Oceania is as anchored in reality as Lilliput, though this later journey is not in space but in time, a trip into the threatening future, an extrapolation of trends already present in contemporary society. Lilliputian politics at first seem outlandish; scrutinized more closely, it is England diminished by twelve. Oceania, similarly, is not the demented antithesis of England but what England may so fearfully become unless the rescue begins now.

Brobdingnag appropriately dwarfs Lilliput as the giant influence. Gulliver and Winston are forever at risk. In the land of the giants Gulliver lives in constant danger from the most banal events of everyday life—the prey of rats, dogs, and monkeys. Trifles, literal and culinary, threaten him: drowning in the soup, stifling in the cream, falling from the table, being pecked to death by birds or stung to it by bees. In the land of the spies Winston risks momentary annihilation from equally petty causes. The wrong expression may be facecrime, and even one's back is not secure, for a vigilant telescreen may detect dorsal dissidence. Details are deadly. Passing a man on the street whose face fleetingly twitches, Winston knows he has seen a corpse, for the culprit is as good as dead. It is a nervewracking society where buying a diary or admiring a paperweight means extinction, where an ink stain on a finger is a death sentence. Beauty is incriminating. Just after his first diary entry, Winston's doorbell rings, and, agonizingly, he has to choose between smudging the pages or leaving them accusingly open. Every instant is imperiled: a glance of the eye, a movement of the limbs, a facial grimace, a word spoken in sleep—any one could be fatal. Compounding this is the total abolition of privacy; the lavatory is the place surest to be under surveillance. Oceania is an exposed society with no reprieving darkness.

That Brobdingnag and Oceania are unusually dangerous societies is most vividly dramatized in the rat incidents. Rats are unpleasant but, the spreading of disease apart, not normally killers. But Brobdingnag is not normal. The manikin is in danger of being devoured alive by giant rats; had he forgotten his sword, he would surely have perished. Winston has no sword, and Room 101 is as abnormal as Brobdingnag, yet frighteningly it is also normal, an established agency of Oceanic rehabilitation and every dissident's assured destination. In Big Brother's slums rats eat helpless babies; Winston is equally helpless, and the rats know it. Looking through Gulliver's eyes, Winston sees "enormous" rats, Brobdingnagian rats, predators, killers. Oceania is finally far more menacing than Brobdingnag; there can be escape from the land of the Giant King but not from that of Big Brother.

The voyage to Brobdingnag molds Winston's attitudes throughout his tale, most explicitly in his reaction to the proles but more generally in the disgust and fear he habitually experiences. The account of his typical workday in the Ministry of Truth just as clearly evinces a debt to Gulliver's third voyage, specifically to the Academy of Lagado and the island of the sorcerers. Winston's job as a confuser of truth—he cannot even be described as a forger since he simply substitutes one piece of nonsense for another—recalls certain vocations pursued in the Academy, except that there they were zanily comic and here they are grimly effective.[2] Millions of pairs of boots are produced on paper while half the population of Oceania goes barefoot; books are turned out by machines while the fields are cultivated with horse ploughs. It sounds similar to the sabotaged land of Balnibarbi and its factitious dearth, sad consequence of a parallel enthrallment to an equally destructive ideology.[3]

Winston's torment at being excluded from truth echoes Gulliver's similar frustration in the third voyage. Winston's job brings him into contact with the whole machinery of mendacity: faked photographs, imitation voices, garbled versions of classic works issued as definitive texts, the manipulation of language. There is no fun in any of this, but neither is there in Gulliver's anguish over official history as a maze of lies. Gulliver's only access to truth is through a sorcerer and the testimony of ghosts; dead men, unlike the living, have no motive to lie.[4] Winston has no means of summoning truth-telling spirits. A liar by profession, he is fated to live amid lies without any hope of hearing truth spoken or recognizing it if it were. Where comedy occurs in Orwell, it is of a disturbingly astringent type, teetering on the edge of *saeva indignatio*. The idiotic Parsons, praising the miracles of economic production while trying to cadge a razor blade, is funny, a perfect candidate for Lagado; yet on reflection such folly is no laughing matter.

Certainly there is little comic relief in the first six chapters, which show Winston at home, at work, lunching in the Ministry canteen, and, courtesy of the diary, having sex with an aging, toothless prole prostitute. It is a thoroughly bleak picture of everyday Oceanic life— its housing, employment, food, and sex. With Chapter Seven an element of hope, however Delphic, appears in the first extended analysis of the proles and their position within Oceania. Swift remains the major influence, but there are hints of another master, albeit one whom Orwell regretfully came to reject (*CEJL*, 2:166–72). Just as Winston's view of himself as the one sane man in a world of lunatics recalls H. G. Wells's *The Country of the Blind*, so Winston's ambivalent attitude to the proles is evocative of the hero's response to the Morlocks in *The Time Machine*. There is, of course, nothing in Orwell's text akin to the indolent Eloi, and the Morlocks are much further down some regressive evolutionary road than the proles will ever be. Nevertheless, Winston follows the Party line in regarding the proles as less than human, a species of inferior animals. Simultaneously fascinated and disgusted, he is drawn irresistibly toward their habitat yet alienated by what he finds there. In Chapter Eight he becomes a practical ethologist, forsaking abstract reflection for empirical verification, going among the proles as Gulliver among the Yahoos, observing their behavior at first hand and in brute detail.

His yearning for a prole rising is the more intense because of his pessimistic conclusion that the Party cannot be overthrown from within. One short paragraph provides five increasingly desperate "ifs" buttressed by two "musts"—surely sooner or later the proles must revolt? More a plea than a question, it cedes to the final dispiriting qualification: "And yet—!" (p. 58). The triumph of hope over experience screeches to a grating halt. *Reasoning* is too honorific a term to apply to these desperate musings. The proles must rebel because otherwise Big Brother is insuperable; the trouble is that there is not a shred of evidence to support this prospect.

It is all too easy to see why the revolutionary pines so ardently for it. He sees simultaneously an iniquitous system and a force certain to shatter it if suitably activated. When nothing happens, the revolutionary often seeks, like Shelley, an explanation in a metaphor of sleep:

> Rise like lions after slumber
> In unvanquishable number—
> Shake your chains to earth like dew
> Which in sleep had fallen on you—
> Ye are many—they are few.[5]

Precisely. The proles are 85 percent of the population of Oceania, yet the Party—worse, the tiny Inner Party—exercises absolute control. Orwell had already engaged the mystery in *Animal Farm* where he suggests, more pessimistically than Shelley, that mere animal power, however great, will always be duped by superior cunning; the mighty horse is doomed to be the prey of the weaker but devious pigs.

Winston fluctuates between reverence and revulsion for the proles. In more sanguine moments he admires them, identifying them as humanly superior to the masters who despise them. What he never sees is a likelihood of rebellion. He hopes, but in vain: the proles are not rebels. He remembers the animal cry of rage in the street, how his heart had leaped to think that the proles were "breaking loose" at last (p. 58). The expression is ominous, suggesting beasts rather than human beings, and so it proves. The "mob" of women in the street market are rioting over a shortage of saucepans, indifferent to the abominations of Big Brother. The disciplined, concentrated fury needed for social revolution is dissipated in a scatter of futile, individual quarrels. They are antagonists, competitors. Two bloated women, hair coming down, wrestle squalidly over the same saucepan and break it: they are unseemly, undignified, stupid. Winston watches in disgust, wondering why such strength must always be squandered on trivia; if only the proles would fight for what mattered. But here is the impasse: the proles cannot rebel until they become conscious and cannot become conscious until they rebel (*CEJL*, 3:279).

So jaundiced a view of the inert, apolitical masses must lead to despair. The proles are inconsequential. Provided they work and breed, they can be left alone, turned loose like cattle to roam at will. Their lives are assigned to sex, beer, and gambling; they go to work at twelve years, marry at twenty, are middle-aged at thirty, dead at sixty. "To keep them in control was not difficult" (p. 59). Their few able members are vaporized; the rest grumble about incidentals, blind to the larger evils that afflict them. Big Brother's tolerance is an insult: why brainwash creatures without brains? No Party member is above suspicion and every prole beneath it. They can do as they please because nothing they do matters; they are free because they are futile. Seconding the embittered Winston is his embittered creator, writing despondently, not about Airstrip One but about the depressing politics of his own time.

The excursion into the prole district, a composite nightmare in which Brobdingnag, Struldbruggs, and Yahoos are all come again, confirms the truth of these sad speculations. Walking their streets, Winston is torn between wish and fact: hope in the proles is both mystical truth and palpable absurdity. The proles are urbanized Yahoos, swarming in astonishing numbers: nubile, crudely painted girls pursued by youths; swollen, waddling women revealing the girls ten years hence; old, bent creatures shuffling along; savage, barefoot children scattering at their mothers' yells. There are no men; it is early evening, and the pubs are packed. The area matches its denizens: decaying buildings, stagnant puddles, and, most ominous, battered doorways curiously suggestive of rat holes. In a book where the rat is the tyrant's ally, it is a damaging association, boding ill for a prole rebellion. Gulliver's nausea at Brobdingnagian flesh and Yahoo bestiality recurs in Winston's revulsion from the pullulating, vermin-like life of the slums, with its rampant sexuality and unsavory inhabitants. These crumbling tenements and squalid lives are those of any English city of the 1930s transported to Airstrip One half a century on.

Gulliver's sense of impotence as he writhes vainly in the hands of the Brobdingnagian maids of honor, in loathsome submission to the giant flesh, is hinted at as Winston observes the "monstrous" women of the slums. It is, significantly, the prole women who provoke this sense of massiveness in Winston: "two monstrous women with brick-red forearms" pause in their inane chatter to watch Winston with animal wariness (p. 68). It is a meeting not of human beings but of alien life-forms.

The greatness of the *Travels* springs from the art with which Swift fused two hitherto disparate themes: *le mythe animal* and the voyage of discovery. Gulliver travels to unearth the shocking truth: man is Yahoo, a species of animal incapable of amendment by precept or example. Winston is a time-traveler, situated in a strange future country that could so easily become our own, and Orwell similarly exploits *le mythe animal* to expose the hopelessness of Winston's predicament. The animal nature of the proles is confirmed in their instinctive prescience of the rocket attack. Amid yells of warning, people shoot into doorways like rabbits, the doorways recently described as rat holes. But, rats or rabbits, threatening or timid, the proles are repeatedly rendered in animal imagery. Nor is it just a metaphor. The proles do possess an instinct, some in-built early warning system, that alerts them to weapons traveling faster than sound. Sometimes the animal is privileged and enjoys advantages that the rational creature lacks. Winston cannot hear the approaching rocket, but he trusts the proles' advice and saves himself.

Winston confronts the proles as Gulliver does the Yahoos; far from recognizing them as equal, he cannot accept them as human. His subsequent reverence for the prole washerwoman is missing on his tour of the slums. He has no respect for this life and certainly none for this death. Coming upon the severed hand of the rocket victim, "he kicked the thing into the gutter." He may call it human but does not treat it so. Within minutes of the explosion, normalcy is restored: "the sordid swarming life of the streets was going on as if nothing had happened" (p. 69). We are not being invited to admire this resilience. "Sordid" is clearly condemnatory, "swarming" scarcely less so; Julia later remarks that parts of London are swarming with rats (p. 118). At the close of *Keep the Aspidistra Flying* Gordon Comstock has a vision of the throbbing, human vitality of London streets;[6] in *Nineteen Eighty-Four* it is a vision of vermin.

When Winston turns to examine the males of the species, this same impression of intense animal activity in a confined space persists. The pubs are "choked" with customers, their grimy doors constantly swinging to and fro. Swift's Giant King, from his Olympian eminence, would have viewed this as the scurrying of the little odious vermin he had pronounced men to be.[7] Without being Olympian, Winston's scrutiny is equally unfavorable. It is curious that Brobdingnagian massiveness should be restricted to the women. The men have somehow shrunk to Winston's size, and he does not feel so claustrophobic in their presence. But he feels just as alienated. The "choked" pubs, smelling of urine, sawdust, and sour beer, compel us to ponder the creatures for whom this is recreation, the highest pleasure that life affords.

Their intellectual pabulum matches their revolting beverage and social intercourse. The men who live unprotestingly in such streets and drink in such dens are mentally attuned to them. Winston comes upon a threesome absorbed in a newspaper: "it was obviously some serious piece of news" (p. 70)—serious enough for them to come to blows. In fact it is far more trivial than the saucepans over which their females squabbled. Saucepans are real and useful, even if they rank lower than personal dignity and a free society. The prole men are wrangling over a pipe dream, a fantasy, over the Lottery, a state-run swindle in which huge imaginary prizes are won by nonexistent persons. It is "the one public event to which the proles paid serious attention"—"the principal if not the only reason for remaining alive" for millions of proles throughout Oceania (p. 70). People unable to read or write are inspired by greed to staggering feats of memory and calculation. Even were prizes and prizewinners real, it would be depressing; that the whole lottery is a lie simply worsens despair. What waste and folly: it is Orwell's judgment as well as Winston's.

There is no hope in the proles; what other verdict is possible? Yet despite the abundant disconfirmations, Winston cleaves to his desperate creed: "But if there was hope, it lay in the proles. You had to cling on to that" (p. 71). *Credo quia impossibile est.* All the evidence is suppressed as Winston exalts faith above experience, dogma above sense. That imbecilic pauper, Parsons, had similarly praised Big Brother's economic miracles, but with one major difference. Parsons is simply a blatant, unmitigated fool. Winston's folly is in a good cause; we all want Big Brother overthrown, and wishes can so easily become convictions. To live without hope is to forfeit humanity.

But if we do hope, it must be against the text. Winston admits that what sounds reasonable as a proposition becomes an act of faith when carried into the street. Are those in Lagado who dream of extracting sunshine from cucumbers any more deluded?[8] When Gulliver first hears of the Struldbruggs, he is ecstatic: immortality is, a priori, a boon, and those born to live forever must be happy. How could it be otherwise? Experience teaches him better; meeting them, he realizes how accursed these poor wretches are; no proposition, however plausible, can survive such empirical exposure.[9] The prole rebellion is, within the text, mere wish fulfillment. We may, of course, point out that the only textual evidence is what Winston provides and argue that he is an unreliable witness. But that too is a literary, not a political, question. We must not assume he is unreliable because his testimony is displeasing. Perhaps Orwell had no intention of pleasing us any more than Swift meant to please *vous autres.*[10] To object that we do not like the presentation of the proles is to risk the snub that Jacques invites when he complains against Rosalind's name: "There was no thought of pleasing you when she was christen'd."[11] Even as Winston entertains his irrational hope, he hears ahead "a din of shouting voices," those of the rowdy, drunken, hopeless people who are supposed to topple Big Brother. What else can this be but subversive irony?

Winston has one more illusion to lose, one more dream to founder. He advances it in the form of yet another conditional: "If there was anyone still alive who could give you a truthful account of conditions in the early part of the century, it could only be a prole" (p. 71). Once again another promising hypothesis proves totally unsound when tested. Winston's Oceanic Nestor turns out to be an Oceanic Struldbrugg. Nor can we argue that Winston was just unlucky in his choice of prole. In a text whose characters are representatives, types even more than individuals, the old prole tells Winston what every old prole will tell him. To object that Winston asked the wrong man is really a disguised dislike of the answers; they are, nevertheless, the only answers available.

In the prole pub Winston finds the English poor of the thirties transplanted to Airstrip One. The beer comes in liters, but little else has changed. Indeed the old prole is still implausibly demanding pints, not because he is Rip Van Winkle but to allow Orwell to contrast old and new. A pint was the measure when the old man was young, but, as the barman sarcastically remarks, "'When you were a young man, we were all living in the treetops'" (p. 72). Allowing for the hyperbole, this is Party orthodoxy. Before the Revolution all was darkness and ignorance; the Party brought enlightenment and liberation to the people. To verify the truth of this claim Winston has come to this insanitary hovel with its "hideous cheesy smell of sour beer," its glasses crudely rinsed in a bucket under the counter, its residents eyeing him suspiciously before returning to the crucial business of the Lottery. In Orwell's depressing diptych of prole life, the squalid female panel of the street scene is now complemented by the equally squalid male panel of the pub.

The conversation from which Winston expected so much turns out to be as disappointing as Gulliver's with the Struldbruggs. Of course, the expectations are exorbitant. The proles, young and old, have no talent for analysis, comparison, or criticism. Winston does admittedly get some snippets of information damaging to Ingsoc. Before the Revolution, says the old man, the beer was better. Even so trifling a heresy cannot be tolerated by the fanatical ideologues of Ingsoc; on small things, great things depend. Once concede that two plus two equals four, and the whole of Ingsoc is undermined; once admit that beer has deteriorated, and who knows where it may end? The old man also remembers wearing a top hat at a long-dead relative's funeral, yet Party history teaches that only capitalists were allowed to wear this article. Winston, keeping his temper, explains patiently that top hats are not important. But why isn't it useful to the dissident to catch the Party in a lie?

Winston is unimpressed. For him the old man's memory is "a rubbish-heap of details" (p. 75). But if you do not like details, you should not talk to proles. Exorbitant expectations breed a correspondingly extravagant despair. Winston wants clinical, conceptual comparison and loses heart when he does not get it. The old man, prompted, recalls an encounter with a drunken "toff" when he threatened to call the police. If, as Ingsoc teaches, the pre-Revolution police were simply the tool of the upper class, the threat would be absurd. Perhaps it is, underscoring the prole's foolish trust in justice, since he, not the aggressor, would have ended up in the cells. But that is clearly not what he believed, though Party apologists might easily ascribe this to sheer ignorance.

Winston thinks he has wasted his time: "A sense of helplessness took hold of Winston" (p. 75). Behind the episode lies Gulliver's disillusionment with the Struldbruggs. Idealized in advance as storehouses of wisdom and experience, they can tell him nothing and spend the interview soliciting handouts. The old prole is no panhandler, but he drinks Winston's beer and makes the most meager of returns. In one last despairing attempt to get him to focus, Winston asks if life was better then or now, but the prole penchant for irrelevant particulars, the inability to take an overall view, is too entrenched. Pompously misunderstanding the question, the old man goes sententiously astray in pointless chatter about the relief of not needing women any more. Winston understandably decides "it is no use going on" and makes his escape as his companion shuffles off to "the stinking urinal." This conclusion unites the two aspects of prole life emphasized throughout the chapter: its futility and its filth.

The hypothesis has been tested and refuted. Party members cannot tell the truth because of brainwashing; the proles are just as impotent but for different reasons. The first cannot recognize, the second cannot formulate, truth: "They remembered a million useless things . . . but all the relevant facts were outside the range of their vision" (p. 76). Allowing for Winston's chagrin, it is not an unjust assessment. Prole truth is not serviceable to a political dissident; Winston will have to forge his anti-Ingsoc ideology without their direct help—but not without their indirect, unconscious contribution.

Among the million useless things dismissed by Winston is "the expression on a long-dead sister's face," and a more enlightened Winston will come to appreciate how indispensably human some "useless" things are: the gestures of love, the paperweight, a sense of beauty, an awareness of tragedy. A far less censorious Winston learns to value the prole contact with everyday life and concrete reality rather than with abstract conceptualization. Thinking of his own futile, fearful obsession with history and the need to change it, he suddenly intuits the superiority of the proles as human beings. Intellectuals waste their lives in ideas and abstractions, bloodless eidolons, inevitably devaluing the discreteness of things and the primacy of individual relationships. The proles do not worship history and care nothing for being lifted clean out of its stream—the chilling threat of O'Brien that strikes terror into Winston's core. What matters to the proles are private loyalties, personal emotions, certain gestures that have no "historical" significance: a tear, an embrace, a word spoken to a dying man. The proles are all little platooners; they know each other, not humanity.[12] The lifeboat-woman is not trying to alter history; she is protecting a child. "The proles had stayed human. . . . They had held on to the primitive emotions which he himself had to re-learn by conscious effort" (p. 134). It is an intellectual's mea culpa. Judged by this criterion, even a lost bicycle pump may have more human significance than the materialist conception of history, and the gestures of love mean more to us as individuals than the great abstractions—race, class, economics, and the rest—which reduce us to ciphers. No abstraction is higher than life, and any abstraction claiming to be so is an idol. The proles have no idols; they live in material squalor but emotional sanity. It is Winston and his co-intellectuals who inhabit a manic world of nightmarish dehumanization. The chastened Winston recalls how callously he kicked the severed hand into the gutter and expresses his contrition for having despised his uneducated fellows: "'The proles are human beings. . . . We are not human'" (p. 134). Ingsoc is stood on its head.

If this revelation strikes Winston like a blow, the attentive reader is better prepared. It is, after all, the prole woman who objects to the obscenity of showing atrocities to children; the Party ranks approve and applaud. No sooner has Syme dismissed the proles as not human than we are shown the young Party executive, quacking like a duck, blank discs instead of eyes; even Winston, despite sharing Syme's sentiment, concludes that "this was not a human being but some kind of dummy" (p. 46). What prole, however degraded, could be worse than this? Winston's frightful choice between the prole prostitute and his appalling wife is one that no man could wish, but a majority might prefer the prostitute; she exploits sex but does not denature it. Even a filthy Yahoo scuffle is better than inhuman mechanization. That the proles use scent and double beds are pluses in a society gripped by a perverted hatred of sex and bodies. The proles, admittedly, succumb to the Hate Song, but only temporarily; just before the arrest, Winston hears the prole mother singing the sentimental love song, and we learn that it has outlived the other. If not ideal, it is unquestionably superior. It vulgarizes a high human emotion, but it displaces a sickening surrender to sadism, the lowest emotion of all. The preference is faultless; between humanity debased and wanton inhumanity, the choice is clear.

On the edge of arrest Winston has a mystical vision of the unconquerable prole mother, inured to hardship and exploitation, indomitably singing, a universal figure to be found all over the world. Yet here too ambivalence lurks. Beneath the high compliment is a latent insult. The victory Winston anticipates will come, it seems, from a future union of mind and matter, with dissident intellectuals fertilizing the fallow strength of the mindless masses. The proles can be trusted to preserve the body; the dissident must keep alive the mind until masculine mind begets upon feminine body the child of revolution. It is simply a variant of the dream demolished in *Animal Farm*, the folly of believing that when clever pig joins mighty horse, the days of exploitation are over. What the fable irrefutably demonstrates is that if the horse has only his strength, he must become the dupe of his astute ally. Even if Big Brother could be overthrown by Winston's desired combination, it would but clear the ground for a new elite and a new tyranny.

But the speculation is extratextual and impermissible. There will be no new elite because the present elite is invincible. Winston *is* the last man in Oceania. There will be no prole rebellion; their very merits preclude it. The qualities that save them from worshipping history make them perpetual dupes; their wholesome concentration on the specificities of the present blinds them to the general requirements of the future. Immersed in the now, they are heedless of the morrow. The little platoon is indifferent to the rest of the army. A prole rebellion is simply another of Winston's delusions, delicious to imagine but impossible to implement. To protest that the proles are better than Big Brother is true but irrelevant. Boxer is nobler than Napoleon, but we know who goes to the knacker. It is not what we want to happen, but what has that to do with it? "From the proletarians nothing is to be feared. Left to themselves, they will continue from generation to generation and from century to century, working, breeding, and dying, not only without any impulse to rebel, but without the power of grasping that the world could be other than it is. . . . They can be granted intellectual liberty because they have no intellect" (p. 166). This is the depressing summation of Goldstein's book, and nothing in Orwell's book rebuts it. Admittedly O'Brien later tells Winston that Goldstein's program for overthrowing Big Brother involves the preposterous notion of a prole rebellion. How Goldstein reached so startling a conclusion is one of the minor unexplained mysteries of *Nineteen Eighty-Four*; it would have made fascinating reading to see how it was done.

The novel's despairing conclusion establishes yet another link with the author of *Gulliver's Travels* and *A Modest Proposal*, but it is equally important to note the divergences as well as the resemblances between Orwell and Swift. A major difference is that Orwell is a divided man, where Swift takes a single, coherent view of the world. Swift never suggests that physical nature is either beautiful or consolatory. For him the human body and the physical world are invariably sources of disgust and discomfiture. He never seeks a solution in nature because, for him, nature is the problem.

Orwell's is a much more complex position. Addicted to Swift from the eve of his eighth birthday when he stole and furtively read the copy of the *Travels* intended for him, Orwell was clearly drawn to the great Augustan by a need to refute the Swift in himself, the fifth columnist within (*CEJL*, 2:39, 4:257, 259–60). Hence his ambivalent fascination for the *Travels*, which he can describe, almost simultaneously, as a near-insane blasphemy against life and as one of a handful of irreplaceable masterpieces produced by Western man, a test of our trusteeship, to be preserved whatever else we might be forced to relinquish. The essay he wrote on Swift reveals a division in Orwell between the democratic optimist who insists that ordinary life is worth living and the Swiftian pessimist obsessed with the vile and the sordid, between the celebrant and the censurer. *Keep the Aspidistra Flying* enacts a conflict between these two selves, ending in victory for the former. *Nineteen Eighty-Four* shows the darker self gaining the upper hand.

But even here the other, sunnier Orwell is not completely silenced. The idyllic visit to the Golden Country with its praise of pastoralism would be inconceivable in Swift, as would the subversive beauty of the naked Julia, shattering a repressive culture in one splendid act of disrobing. In Swift the naked body is always presented in a context of loathing and condemnation. Orwell's nude heroine recalls, rather, Milton's Eve or Blake's human form divine: "the nakedness of woman is the work of God."[13] Orwell dissents from Swift in finding much to revere in nature: the sweet air of the pastoral interlude and the still sweeter song of the thrush that the lovers hear in hushed adoration. About to be arrested, Winston escapes his caste conditioning to see for the first time the beauty of the prole woman as the once "monstrous" form is metamorphosed into "that valiant figure in the yard" (p. 173). Even in Oceania beauty endures: handsome diary, beautiful paperweight, maternal and sexual love, the excursion to the Golden Country, Julia's nakedness, the thrush's song, the unconquerable prole mother. We shall scour Swift in vain for any equivalents.

But just as undeniably *Nineteen Eighty-Four* is a Swiftian book, with nature invoked to demean as well as to exalt. It is a book crowded with disgust and fear: on the one hand, urine, sawdust, sour beer, crumbling cigarettes, firewater gin, the reek of sweat, dust in the creases of face, blocked drains, stew that looks like vomit; on the other, broken bones, smashed teeth, bloody clots of hair, gorilla-like guards, detailed descriptions of hangings, the tremor of terror that thrills Winston's bowels. Orwell criticized "Swift's endless harping on disease, dirt and deformity" (*CEJL*, 4:260). It seems a strange complaint from the creator of Oceania, almost as if he had succumbed to the doublethink he lambasted.

From the outset human beings are compared to porpoises, tiger cubs, beetles, monkeys, rats, rabbits. The ugliness of everyday life is almost monotonously emphasized: the sweaty shorts turned inside out; Parsons, nasally present even when he is miles away; the little, scuttling beetle-like men who "proliferate" in the Ministries; bugs, dirty clothes, and villainous cheap scent in the prole quarters where women swarm, eager to sell themselves for a glass of gin; the coarseness of the toothless prostitute pulling up her skirt. London is a dingy city of underfed people, crumbling houses, bad lavatories, the ubiquitous smell of cabbage. O'Brien's elegant apartment is the one oasis of beauty in a squalid urban wasteland. People rot with the buildings. Winston observes with fascinated abhorrence the decomposing body of the once-titanic Rutherford, now a corpse waiting to be sent to the grave; Julia complains about always living in the stink of women; the vomiting prole woman is the wreck of a once-impressive physique; Parsons excretes into the defective pan; Winston belches through purple, alcoholic lips.

Much of this loathsomeness is man-made, presumably capable of being ameliorated or abolished. But far more disconcerting, much of it seems just as surely rooted in nature and would continue even if Big Brother were overthrown and a decent political system established. At the height of summer, "the stench of the Tubes at the rush hours was a horror" (p. 120). Just as Orwell's protest against political execution modulates into a musing on the mystery of death itself, so his attack upon an evil political regime deepens into an anguish at the ineradicable defects of human life. Even in the just society man remains, at least intermittently, a Yahoo.

The animal associations bring fear as well as hope. Nature is ambiguous, equivocal, duplex. The book opens in a "vile" wind. As the lovers listen ecstatically to the thrush, a little beetle man may be listening too. Balancing Julia's naked beauty is Winston's ruined reflection in the mirror. Division and dichotomy are the truth of existence. Winston dislikes nearly all women, especially the young and pretty ones, yet in his dream of the Golden Country the leaves of the trees stir in dense masses like women's hair, a highly attractive image. The split is in life as much as in Winston. Nature is double: thrush and beetle, beautiful and loathsome, consoler and destroyer. The Golden Country is bathed in sunlight, dappled with pools of gold. Surely sunlight is unreservedly on the side of the angels. Yet in Room 101 Winston imagines himself in the middle of a great empty plain, a flat desert drenched with sunlight, across which all sounds came out of immense distances. Sunlight has gone over to the torturer; nature has become alien, hostile, inhuman. The final chapter opens with Winston seated at his usual table in the Chestnut Tree in a ray of sunshine, but it brings neither comfort nor reassurance, holds no Wordsworthian promise; there is no salvation in nature. Appallingly there is damnation. The rat, the worst thing in the world, comes not out of politics but out of nature. It is not a political abomination but a natural evil; it predates Ingsoc and will survive should Ingsoc ever fail. We imagined we knew what was most intolerable about Oceania: that it is a floodlit society, exposed to unremitting inspection, the place where there is, tragically, no darkness. We had come to regard darkness as friendly, reprieving. Now out of darkness comes the rat, the supreme nocturnal terror, the prince of darkness, to demoralize the hero. Nothing, finally, can save Winston: neither the private life nor the public, politics nor nature, light nor darkness. A Swiftian conclusion to a Swiftian book.

And yet all this, important though it be, leaves the major debt to Swift unacknowledged, for it is essentially a matter not of individual borrowings but of a complete structural appropriation. Still insufficiently recognized is the degree to which *Nineteen Eighty-Four* is shaped by Swift's great fable, how, in wrestling with the central problem of the *Travels*—the hunt for the human being—Orwell came to create his own dark masterpiece.

Both texts pursue the truth about man, seeking the true self beneath the accretions of culture and the drapings of mythology; both end in a kind of conversion in which once-sacrosanct dogmas about human identity are exposed as untenable superstitions. Gulliver travels to all those far places and meets all those strange peoples to confront not the external world but the reality within: he is his own greatest, most appalling discovery. What he finds shatters the smug assumption enshrined in the logic manuals: *homo est animal rationale.*[14] The pool in Houyhnhnmland, where he sees his own face, reveals a very different, nauseating reality. Winston is similarly taken to Room 101 not to learn the truth of Oceania but of himself, to be broken with the disclosure of his own turpitude. Big Brother remains a mystery; it is Winston who is stripped bare. In each case there is the same reaction: after such knowledge, what forgiveness? The search for the self, whether in comic satire or somber prophecy, ends in catastrophic success; the educated hero confronts his shamefulness in Houyhnhnmland and Oceania alike.

Swift seeks to intimidate and demoralize; he induces a fearful questioning of what it means to be human, verging upon a panic-stricken intuition that it may mean nothing at all. No reader of the *Travels* can miss the theme of conditioning and entrapment that informs the whole fiction. For many centuries we in the West have celebrated the autonomous self as the supreme value, so precious that we continue to reject solutions to our most grievous social problems when they threaten the sanctity of individual rights. The earthly paradise itself comes too dear if the cost is the suppression of the self.

The Darker Self

Gulliver's Travels shockingly proposes that this exalted idea of the self, cornerstone of Christianity and humanism alike, is mere delusion. As Gulliver moves from society to society, to be molded anew to each fresh set of cultural assumptions, the nihilistic speculation becomes increasingly insistent: perhaps ultimately there is no self, no central human core beyond the reach of manipulation, no human defense against the coercions of culture. Such satire puts on trial the very existence of the self as an entity independent of the social system in which it acquires awareness. What is so unnerving about Gulliver is that he changes so easily with each change of environment; he is a chameleon, an essentially relative creature. Man, in the sense of some irreducibly human core, some residuum transcending cultural control, resisting or modifying environmental omnipotence, is shown as a fiction, the belief that there is a human given exposed as the most pathetic of delusions.

The scandal of Swift is his suggestion that man is merely a mechanism, a function of his environment, imprisoned in a system that he evades, if at all, only to enter another, forever exchanging captivities. Gulliver travels, demonstrating that the same belief may be truistic or ludicrous depending on its social context and that what some call truth, others call prejudice; he demonstrates too how easily man can be reconditioned to abhor what he once revered and to regard as normal what was formerly bizarre. But if man is so infinitely malleable, so much a moral and intellectual weathervane, what becomes of the boasted freedom of the mind, the inviolable sanctity of the self? What makes the *Travels* so chillingly modern is its anticipation of a major theme of structuralism in suggesting that man is simply the sum of his codes, programmed to follow instructions, incapable of change, until reprogramming occurs. There is no self apart from society, no nature but only culture, no freedom but only conditioning.

Yet far from putting down the *Travels* convinced that all is relative and contingent, the reader is only too disturbingly aware that the search for the self has ended in the absolute fact of Yahoo man. Appearing to discredit all truth, the book ends in this distressing, inescapable truth. The Yahoo is real; it is the rational qualities we pride ourselves on that are exposed as spurious. This is the truth that Swift sends Gulliver traveling to learn. He sets out on his final voyage secure in certain unimpugnable facts: that England is the queen of nations and man the crown of creation, that society, with all its institutions and artifacts, is the attestation of human excellence. In Houyhnhnm-land he is made aware of the frauds practiced upon him: man is not *animal rationale* but Yahoo; society reflects not the flattering proofs of human achievement but the evidence of human depravity.

Winston Smith is engaged on a similar search, which culminates in a similar disaster. He too strives to fathom the mystery of his own being by ransacking his memory, by engaging old proles in pub conversations in the hope of deciphering history, by treasuring every scrap of evidence from the abolished past. He desperately seeks confirmation of what he already knows is true: that truth is objective, existing regardless of the fears and wishes of men, that love is stronger than hate, that the skull is an inviolable realm, a no-go area to the strongest conceivable tyrant, that the past is unalterable with yesterday's events beyond recall or revision. These are the adamantine truths upon which Winston relies as he initiates his challenge to Big Brother. From the outset he is prepared for the worst, and the worst is that he will be caught, tortured, and executed. But he knows too that the truths he cherishes are insuperable and that when his body is dead his ideals will triumph.

Nineteen Eighty-Four records an education as Winston is taught, painfully, to discard these errors for harsher but correct views. The autonomous self, truth, love, generosity, and friendship are all pipe dreams; Orwell, campaigning against the infantilism that will not abide unpleasant facts, reserves the harshest fact of all for his final utterance. Winston's final transformation is as shocking as Gulliver's. Gulliver switches from lover of humanity to misanthrope, Winston from freedom fighter to power worshipper, rebel to lickspittle. Each ends by denying values once cherished, becoming renegade to all previously held dear. Yet each author makes it impossible for us simply to repudiate the renegade for deserting the great tradition to which we still unswervingly belong. It would neuter these books to present them as serene affirmations of the values that their protagonists so scandalously renounce. Gulliver and Winston go wrong in a way that makes it very difficult to eschew their company. The beliefs they reject are ours too, among our most prized possessions, and it is inconceivable that their creators expect us to follow these defectors all the way, abandoning wives for stables or loving our violators. Why, then, do Swift and Orwell impede readers when they understandably try to extricate themselves from a compromising involvement with the traitors? At what point in these narratives can we, without being smug or pharisaical, dissociate ourselves from their heroes' aberrations?

When Gulliver gazes into the pool and sees staring back the face of the Yahoo, he is not just a harmless lunatic inviting our pity or derision; he is our delegate to Houyhnhnmland, and it would be altogether too facile to repudiate him for daring to call us Yahoos. When Winston cracks so shamefully yet so inevitably in Room 101, it is not just an individual lapse but the fall of man. To jib, however justifiably, at the sensationalism of the rats is beside the point. Not the individual instance but the general psychological law is what concerns Orwell; Room 101 is unendurable. For anyone to claim that he could overcome it and that Winston's capitulation proves only his own personal cravenness is to make nonsense of Orwell's intention. Our relationship to Gulliver and Winston is far more problematic than a simple rejection of kinship; they are our brothers, even if the relationship is nothing to celebrate. The fact that we are ashamed and discomfited does not entitle us to pretend that they are strangers. The cupboard holds our skeleton too.

Orwell has built a trap. Winston begins as our spokesman, upholding our verities. When, aping Gulliver, he deserts to the enemy, it sets us a problem. We are not to join him in craven capitulation, but neither can we simply condemn him as a weakling, fallen miserably below our own high standards. To imply that Big Brother's good fortune was not to have us for opponents smacks of presumption. The book asks us to identify with Winston and to say honestly how we would fare in his place. Orwell's mortifying intention within the text is to extort the humiliating confession that we would do no better. The logic of Oceania is that the last man is doomed to defeat, simply because in such a dark finale any hope of individual resistance has vanished. The book is a grim warning not to let things get so bad or else all is lost. Orwell exhorts his readers to act now to prove him wrong. Prevention is the aim, not just because prevention is better than cure but for the far more urgent reason that there is no cure; Oceania is too late for salvation.

We can, if we wish, dismiss Oceania as a bugaboo, a nightmare that our waking state will never countenance, and deny that our world can ever become so bad because there are certain in-built guarantees, certain promises—epistemological, psychological, moral—that veto the possibility of such degradation. But Winston has already said all this and been proved disastrously wrong. Orwell feared Oceania and thought it more likely in proportion as it was discounted. He had not praised the nightmare quality of *Darkness at Noon* to encourage people to rebuke a similar effect in his own novel (*CEJL*, 3:271–72, 275). Liberal protestations notwithstanding, the worst thing in the world can happen; Room 101 is built with the inadvertent planning permission of those who glibly deny its possibility. Winston is, from the start, too optimistic. He fears capture and death but not surrender. He "knows" that the worst cannot happen, that certain nightmarish speculations cannot survive in daylight; his punishment is to see the nightmare become fact in the place where there is no darkness.

Winston's dogmas prove to be delusions, a series of blunders in epistemology and ethics. He believes in the inviolability of truth and love, thereby challenging what Orwell denounced as the two most monstrous of modern iniquities: the denial of objective truth and the growth of power worship. Power is impotent against truth and love; two plus two equals four, whatever Big Brother says to the contrary; Winston loves Julia, and nothing can change that. In mind and heart man is invulnerable. These granite assumptions crumble when put to the test. Winston's root error, the sandy foundation of all his other convictions, is his trust in the sufficient self, his confidence that the individual can always master his environment. "Fool, do not boast, thou canst not touch the freedom of my mind."[15] Milton's Lady, physically trapped, derides her foolish captor; the spirit is free even when the body is shackled.

There is abundant evidence that Orwell agreed with the Lady. Bozo, the crippled pavement artist in *Down and Out in Paris and London,* refuses to be ashamed of a beggary he did not choose and cannot help. The worst degradation, as the organizers of the death camps realized, is that which is appropriated and internalized, when the victim sees himself as vermin. No person is completely victimized until he annuls himself. Bozo will not annul himself. Doubly penalized, lame and poor, he rejects society's evaluation that he is worthless. Scorning environmental servitude, he taps his forehead and insists, "'I'm a free man in here.'"[16] We are all, if we choose, free in there. No matter how vile the world, we need not be its helpless victims, far less its accomplices, for resistance is always our privilege. Even in the most unpropitious circumstance—Parisian slum and English dosshouse, the stricken north of England with its poor huddled in apathetic desolation, the nightmare city of Barcelona given over to witch-hunt—Orwell finds the proofs of man's invincible nobility. Man is at once decent and insuperable; when the world does its worst, he does his best, and his best is always good enough. The decency of ordinary folk is the epiphany that illumines the close of *Keep the Aspidistra Flying;* the blessed permanence of London is the redemptive vision at the end of *Coming Up for Air.* This euphoria culminates in the figure of the Italian soldier in *Homage to Catalonia:* "no bomb that ever burst shatters the crystal spirit" (*CEJL,* 2:303–6). It is Orwell's secular equivalent of the Christian assurance that grace is always sufficient. Consciousness is the lord of being; the mind can control any calamity; the self sustain any challenge. Milton's Lady would have cheered.

She would surely have been perplexed and dismayed by Orwell's last book. How can so shocking a recantation of all that had been so previously cherished be explained? The assurance that society may condition but cannot denature us is revoked; the champion of the crystal spirit seems to have defected to Torquemada. The quondam confidence in unconquerable man is as shattered as the shattered paperweight, and consciousness is now the terrified thrall of being. The humiliated bankrupt of Airstrip One is a world away from Milton's Lady. If, as Boris declares in *Down and Out,* victory goes to him who fights the longest, then it is, scandalously, O'Brien, and not

Winston, who has the staying power (p. 32). If, as Bozo says in *Down and Out*, force is futile against the brave spirit, that spirit is now dismissed as the discredited dogma of an outworn mythology (p. 147). Gordon Comstock's reverence for the tree of life is an anachronism; the Party is about to abolish the orgasm and commence in vitro fertilization. George Bowling's confidence that human nature is too massively and solidly established to be altered is a delusion; there is no human nature, simply a substance malleable as putty in Big Brother's hands.

All Orwell's reiterated rebukes and warnings to the optimists and liberals are now embodied as real, unexorcisable horrors. He had urged the English not to trust the deceptive legacy of liberalism: the empty guarantees that truth must prevail, that persecution must defeat itself, that mental freedom is inviolable—all these beliefs of the nursery that surprise us when still cherished by the political adult. He had identified as a major weakness of English culture the "sentimental belief that it all comes right in the end and the thing you most fear never happens" (*CEJL*, 2:297). Whatever appalls the mind cannot happen is the first article of the liberal creed. By contrast *Nineteen Eighty-Four* nerves itself to imagine the worst and then enacts the horror. From the outset Winston fears that his rebellion is the act of a lunatic, and the book verifies his fears. Room 101 is the harsh school where the defects of a liberal education are corrected.

Why, for example, is H. G. Wells so foolish as to believe that only good people can be good scientists (*CEJL*, 2:169–70)? Perhaps science itself, eugenics in particular, might carry the manipulative threat: "it may be just as possible to produce a breed of men who do not wish for liberty as to produce a breed of hornless cows" (*CEJL*, 1:419). Is the crystal spirit as secure against brainwashing as it is against bombs? The liberal assumes that the human spirit is a constant throughout history, forever threatened but, like Dryden's hind, destined never to die.[17] It is a belief that rests ultimately upon the antihistorical conviction that human nature is an unalterable datum, unvarying from age to age, superior to history and immune to event. From the Enlightenment assumption of a constant human nature to the modern liberal trust in the human spirit as an insuperable check to totalitarianism, this belief has been the cornerstone of Western optimism, shared, as the crystal allusion shows, by Orwell himself.

What if it isn't true? What if man is not a constant? What if love of liberty is merely a cultural artifact, a conditioned reflex that fades as the matrix alters? Slavery cannot endure, declares the liberal; Orwell points to the great slave states of antiquity that lasted for millenia and asks how we can be so sure that they cannot return, this time the more tenaciously because science and technology will support them (*CEJL,* 1:414, 2:298, 3:231). People bred for servitude is a nightmare that an innocent liberalism will not contemplate, but does that mean that it cannot happen? "What sickens me about left-wing people, especially the intellectuals, is their utter ignorance of the way things actually happen" (*CEJL,* 1:395). *Nineteen Eighty-Four* rubs the intellectuals' noses in the dirt they will not see, even when it is sometimes of their own making. "The thing you most fear never happens." What Orwell most feared was the shattering of the crystal spirit; that the speculation was abhorrent was no reason for banning it.

Hence the deliberate affront to the optimists as Orwell goes to the other extreme: they said such horrors cannot happen. Orwell's text shows that they must. Winston is, shockingly, defeated in the mind, precisely where Milton's Lady taunts the torturer that he cannot reach. The past is unchangeable, truth is objective, words have fixed meanings: all of these precious axioms are revealed as hanging on the slenderest filaments. The book shocks because these irrefutable propositions are refuted. "It is quite possible that we are descending into an age in which two and two will make five when the Leader says so" (*CEJL,* 1:413–14). Suspense comes, if at all, not from wondering whether Winston can elude, far less overthrow, Big Brother but whether he can sustain defiance to the modest extent of dying for the faith, winning the martyr's crown: "the object is not to stay alive but to stay human" (p. 136). Even covert martyrdom, a secret disobedience carried to the grave, a hidden heresy, will keep a man human. There is no need for Winston to join Spartacus, More, or Bonhoeffer provided he dies privately hating Big Brother. Yet even this modest victory is a fantasy, as much a piece of wish fulfillment as Jack the

Giant-Killer. The Giant wins; the dissident keeps his life but loses his humanity.

Survival is here a greater calamity than death. Heroic death would be a triumph, an election. Let Winston go to the grave bravely defiant or even stealthily nonconformist and Oceanic totalitarianism is irretrievably flawed, for if even one sheep is lost, the infallible argument of totalitarian pastoralism is ruined. But Winston is "rescued," though in such a way that the unrelinquishable life is more degrading than the unendurable death. The worst thing in the world is that there is no death, only life, in Room 101; Winston, like the Struldbruggs, is condemned to life.

He is denied the gift of heroic, expiatory death because it is now an anachronism, as obsolete as Shakespeare and the paperweight. Humanism is refused even a martyr. What Winston most fears as lunatic, heretic, minority of one, is that there is no truth to die for, and the book confirms his dread. Relying on the spirit of man, Winston might just as well have trusted in Poseidon or the exploded God of Christian mythology. The freedom of the mind is as gross a superstition as the flying house of Loreto, excusable in Milton's Lady, blessedly ignorant of Pavlov and brainwashing, but unforgivable in the residents of Oceania. Man's palimpsest existence, his lack of any authentic human core, leaves him defenseless against the reality in which he lives, moves, and has his being.

Winston's dilemma is identical in ethics as in aesthetics: the things he admires have no future. "We live in an age in which the autonomous individual is ceasing to exist . . . ceasing to have the illusion of being autonomous" (*CEJL*, 2:161). Once man believed himself a free and separate being; the twentieth century taught him better. Oceania rounds off his education by consigning every other humane value to the trashcan. *Nineteen Eighty-Four* is the death certificate of Renaissance man.

Winston's twin nightmares are verified in the end. The first is the epistemological dread of being locked within the self with no access to objective truth or even of knowing if such truth exists. From this it is a fatally easy step to regarding truth as simply the expression of the *führer's* will. It has been said that our ignorance of history makes us slander our own times, causing us to regard them as uniquely dire when they are merely routine. Orwell (who was not ignorant of history) repudiates this nonchalant adoption of modern iniquity. For him, power worship and the denial of objective truth were hideously novel evils, spawned by the twentieth century, unprecedentedly wicked. His book enacts a doomed attempt to escape the misery of contingency by discovering a kingdom, a paradise within, impervious to human manipulations and the arrogance of power. Winston fears that truth has suffered the same fate as law in Oceania. Nothing is illegal in Oceania because there are no laws to break, which means that everything is illegal because there are no laws to keep. Winston shares Orwell's own craving for unalterable law; he dreads a past malleable as putty when he wants one solid as rock. What Omar Khayyam laments—the irreversibility of time and the immutability of event, the moving finger that cannot unwrite what it has written—is what Winston pines for: an irrevocable past, an unrepeatable yesterday, a truth settled forever. Reality, says Winston, is out there, independent of our wishes, and the greatness of the mind is its ability to grasp what is given. Reality, counters O'Brien, is inside the skull, and the skull is the fiefdom of Big Brother: "nothing exists except through human consciousness," and over this the tyrant has total control (p. 210). O'Brien's view prevails.

The associated moral horror is to be walled within the self with no outlet to generosity or love. Winston starts out fearing the epistemological nightmare and ends up trapped in the moral one. Two plus two equals whatever Big Brother decides, and the whole world, Julia especially, can perish provided Narcissus lives. There is no truth of any kind to live or die for except the preciousness of one's squalid self. The paradox is that Winston's self-love is yoked to self-contempt. A person sinks to the pit of degradation when he internalizes the humiliator's judgment. Such was the strategy pursued in the camps. The aim was not simply to make Auschwitz *das Arschloch der Welt* ("the world's arsehole") where human beings were transformed into waste product but to induce the victims to regard themselves as excrement. The victim's sense of his own value must be destroyed within the citadel of his own mind, since whoever harbors his own worth has thwarted the totalitarian enemy. Those who respect themselves will not become Big Brother's lovers.

Consciousness determines being: you are what you resolutely think you are; the reflection in the mirror cannot obliterate the image in the mind. In the Ministry of Love being overwhelms consciousness; spirit capitulates to matter when Winston accepts himself as the bag of filth that O'Brien and the mirror declare him to be. The book appalls to the degree that it fulfills O'Brien's vow to drain Winston of all redemptive nobility. Only the Yahoo remains, sordid, mean, incapable of heroism or self-transcendence. Winston is not the man he thought he was or tried to be, neither dissident nor lover; what possible bearing could his thoughts or strivings have upon his destiny? Others decide what he is; he is O'Brien's wretch, the mere commodity of the system within which he transiently, inconsequentially functions. "Being rules, O.K.," is the dismaying graffito scrawled over Orwell's last communiqué.

The world is barren of truth and love, a dual dispossession that provokes very different reactions. It is shocking to learn that there is no truth because it leaves one feeling cheated; man is mistaken about the universe, but he is not responsible for the world's unreason and may even feel indignant at the world's betrayal. But it is shameful to learn that there is no love, for, if true, that is man's fault; he is the traitor, not the victim. In an absurd world where he alone has value, man can regard himself as victim, even as tragic hero. In a loveless world he must confess himself culprit. That is why Room 101 is the appropriate terminus of this despondent text. It exists to exhibit man as inadequate, even vile, a bag of filth, thereby denying him the tragic status that has hitherto always been his consolation for defeat. Orwell defined tragedy as a destruction in which man nevertheless shows himself greater than the forces that destroy him (*CEJL*, 4:338). Big Brother prohibits heroism; the defeat in Room 101 is indecent, and the tragedy is that it is no tragedy.

Winston and humanism are demolished together. We can, if we wish, soften this conclusion by treating it as the debacle of one very flawed individual whose failure leaves the true doctrine intact, thus wrenching the text away from the despair-of-a-dying-man view to that of a cautionary tale for progressives, an optimistic exhortation to those who share the faith not to ape the blunders. Yet the inadequate Winston is the only liberal champion textually present, the last of his kind, as O'Brien taunts him. Is that in itself an implied judgment on the kind he represents? Orwell attacked *Gulliver's Travels* as a reactionary, pessimistic book, though Swift did at least include Don Pedro as an exception, a partial corrective, to his vision of ubiquitous corruption (*CEJL*, 4:243, 256, 259). There is no Don Pedro in *Nineteen Eighty-Four*, simply torturers and victims, who sometimes switch roles, perplexing us as to which is the more revolting. We may describe Winston as inadequate humanist provided we resist the temptation to import into the text a tougher strain of humanism (our own, naturally), which would have sustained Winston if only he had found it. The related fallacy is to pity poor Winston for not being like us, and it is the graver because he is like us; he is the universal representative. His defects are not those of an individual or a group but, at crucial moments, of humanity itself. The quotation from Lermontov's preface to *A Hero of Our Time*, annexed by Camus to describe his own "hero" in *The Fall*, could just as appositely precede *Nineteen Eighty-Four*; "It is in fact a portrait but not of an individual; it is the aggregate of the vices of our whole generation in their fullest expression."[18] It is much too facile to dismiss Winston as a weakling and think thereby to evade indictment of ourselves, impossible to believe that Orwell means us to escape so easily.

This is so obvious that one wonders how it is ever missed. Of course, Winston is inadequate, compromised, guilty—like everyone else. Condemning him is easy; amending ourselves is more difficult. Take the passage where Winston agrees to commit all manner of atrocities to help overthrow Big Brother, the very atrocities that make Big Brother so detestable in the first place. It is easy to denounce this doublethink, harder to select someone entitled to throw the first stone, for Dresden, Hiroshima, Vietnam, the whole urban guerrilla sprawl, all in some way represent a deal with our own O'Briens and we are all in some degree Winston. To single him out for special censure is as if lepers were to expel a fellow sufferer from their colony.

Making this deal, Winston has already lost the moral chess game awaiting him in the Ministry of Love. O'Brien has him taped and, at a crisis in their confrontation, explodes the claim to moral superiority by playing back the diabolic commitment agreed by the purportedly moral man. The outmatched Winston protests that something in the universe, "'some spirit, some principle,'" will defeat Big Brother (p. 214). O'Brien, for once misreading (deliberately?) Winston's mind, proposes God as the likeliest candidate, only for Winston to disavow the transcendent God of traditional religion. His God is the God of nineteenth-century humanism, the God in man, totally immanent, extradited by Feuerbach from the heaven where his creator, man, in an immature act of self-alienation, had mistakenly exiled him.

The trap is sprung when O'Brien lures Winston into declaring that he too, as man, participates in godhead; if humanity is God, all men are divine. But as the tape recording makes plain, there is nothing morally to distinguish Winston from O'Brien nor, presumably, his God from O'Brien's savage deity. There is no need to dispute Winston's rhetoric when the enemy has on tape the voice of the last, self-proclaimed man swearing to throw acid in a child's face and a full-length mirror to reveal the bag of filth that is the alleged last guardian of the human spirit. Winston's faith, however attractive, fails; the humanist ethos crumbles under presssure: *animal rationale* is the consoling dream, Yahoo the sickening reality. In place of Blake's human form divine, there is a stinking animal, and all three defeats—moral, intellectual, and physical—are interrelated. Winston weeps uncontrollably at the sight of his ruined body because, broken morally and intellectually, he has only the body left, and it is here that the hazards of rejecting transcendence become so evident.

Certainly O'Brien would need a different strategy to subdue, say, an Augustinian Christian who already knows, more than his most maliciously inventive enemy could insinuate, the depth of his corruption. Such a man is presumably insulated against Winston's traumatic experience; to destroy him, you have to surprise him with what he does not know. Unlike Winston he can hurl O'Brien's reply at the mirror: that his personal ruin leaves his God majestic as ever. What makes for pessimism is that these parallel solutions, O'Brien's and the Christian's, are not Orwell's; of the book's three gods, Winston's (and Orwell's) is exposed as the plaster sham. It is his own humanism that Orwell discredits. The physical demolition would be relatively trivial were Winston, like Milton's Lady, morally equipped to handle it, but his anticathartic ruin is sacramental, an outward sign of a complete inward collapse. Yet we must not be too glib in condemning Winston, for he struggles long and suffers terribly. We know this on unimpeachable authority since it is O'Brien himself who says so: "'You are a difficult case. But don't give up hope. Everyone is cured sooner or later'" (p. 217). Everyone. It should make us pause before pharisaically assuming our own impregnability.

The tape is not so disastrously demoralizing as the mirror, for if it condemns Winston as terrorist, it exalts him as lover, prizing love as the best thing in the world. O'Brien, accepting the challenge, introduces the worst thing in the world to test which will prevail. The result is horrendous. Winston savors the full shame of his selfhood and acknowledges the humiliating truth: the bag of filth is the most precious thing in the universe, and he will discard any love, grovel to any abomination, if only the panel restraining the rats stays closed. "If you want to keep a secret you must also hide it from yourself" (p. 223). Room 101 is the confessional where every secret is laid bare. O'Brien refuses to tell Winston how to save himself. No outside agent must intervene, and help is, in any case, redundant, since the self always and infallibly knows what to do. Deaf to Winston's frantic appeals, O'Brien supplies only the simple assurance: "'You will do what is required of you'" (p. 226). Without tuition. And Winston does.

This moment of shameful self-recognition is almost a trademark of modern literature, but its pioneer is the Swift of Gulliver's last voyage, and it was there undoubtedly that Orwell found his inspiration. There is no human nature apart from the acts of men; we are the deed's creatures. Winston is helpless before the demands of self-transcendence. Milton's Lady is superannuated. There is only a flesh reliably feeble and a self dependably insufficient; we do what is required of us. Winston has behaved shamefully, and he could not help it. An inexpiable guilt, a sense of sin so intense that it negates any remedial action: this is the worst torment of all. Sin without God: it is Camus's definition of the absurd.[19] He might easily have had Winston Smith in mind when he framed it.

How can fallen man recover innocence? *Nineteen Eighty-Four* supplies no answer. What it does show is a failure to find absolution, either from oneself or from others. Winston, seared with the shame of his coupling with the prostitute, tries in vain to free himself by writing it away, by exorcising it through the diary: "He had written it down at last, but it made no difference. The therapy had not worked" (p. 58). Confessing one's guilt brings, in itself, no absolution, as Orwell's perjured lovers discover. Each admits betrayal but in such a way as to intensify self-loathing rather than procure pardon or relief. How can we learn to forgive ourselves when the only confessional belongs to the enemy, and one goes there to be degraded, not redeemed? *Nineteen Eighty-Four* explores the humiliation of man, while making it difficult for us to repudiate Winston. At what point did he go wrong? At which test would we have done better? It is a trap as cunning as any set by Swift, for we have been maneuvered into a distressing complicity, which we abjure only at the risk of self-righteousness. It is a representative defeat, with all men falling in Winston as they did in Adam but this time with no redeemer. Even in the *Travels* Gulliver exempts his sextumvirate of moral supermen from the general incrimination, but Orwell ruthlessly denies the possibility of heroism.[20] Winston knows in his dream that his mother and sister must die so that he may live, for this is "part of the unavoidable order of things" (p. 27). Gulliver similarly concludes his catalog of human depravities by telling us that "this is all according to the due course of things."[21] What sensible man will quarrel with reality? Egoism is the law of life. When, no longer dreaming, Winston remembers his mother beseeching him not to be selfish, he remembers too the futility of her appeal: what chance has decency against an empty belly? He snatches all the chocolate and condemns his sister to death. The shame afterward is just another pointless crucifixion, for it is the shame of being human. What else could he have done? The child is father to the man, for he condemns his lover as he did his sister. "'Do it to Julia!'" he screams—as, Orwell implies, we shall all scream when put to the test, interposing our own Julias between us and the horror.

It strikes Winston that "in moments of crisis one is never fighting against an external enemy, but always against one's own body" (p. 84), and it is the pain-shunning body, swelling to fill the universe, that betrays the would-be idealist. In battle the high, noble issues cede to brute preservation. Only those in cosy armchairs dream of self-transcendence; those attended by fear and want know how untamably strong is the animal will to survive. Well-fed people easily control the pangs of hunger. Once again there is a despicably easy escape for any reader determined to dodge the accusation in Orwell's text: to insist that Winston's failure is his own and, as such, no index of our fortitude. When we reach Room 101 we shall show him how it should be done.

Yet the text will not permit us to arraign Winston as sole culprit or isolate him as a sad exception, for he is all too painfully the human representative, our man in Oceania. In the Ministry of Love a skull-faced man, clearly dying of starvation, is given some bread by a fellow prisoner who is at once brutally beaten by a guard for his act of charity; Good Samaritans are bad citizens in Airstrip One. The skull-faced man, ordered to Room 101, begs obscenely for reprieve and in his frantic search for a substitute victim fixes naturally upon his benefactor, hysterically accusing him of having whispered treason as he gave the bread. The Eucharist is polluted. Orwell's rendition of the parable focuses less upon the charity of the Good Samaritan than upon the degrading ingratitude of the recipient. If the greatest love is to die for another, the nadir of selfishness is to use the benefactor's body as a shield.

Nor is the skull-faced man to be regarded as a monster of depravity, for within the text he is a normal man acting as all men do when put to the test, as the Good Samaritan himself will act when summoned to Room 101. We may feel ashamed only on condition that we recognize the guilt as universal. Room 101 is where humanity is found wanting, not where cowards are separated from heroes. In Oceania there are no heroes or martyrs since these are simply the mistakes of an inefficient penology, of blundering executioners who take people at their word that they prefer death when they are really fake suicides, inadvertently killing themselves in an obstinate attempt to make it look real. It is essentially a matter of chronology, of being on hand at the inevitable moment when the "hero" has seen through his own sham and is screaming to be saved from himself. Nothing is finally more important than one's own skin. "'All you care about is yourself,'" says Julia, explaining her treachery as a single instance of a universal law, and Winston, the betrayed betrayer, taught by his own experience, dolefully agrees (p. 232). Orwell's characters do as they must and despise themselves for it, stuck with their shameful selves forever. Even the desperate refuge of hysterical amnesia is denied them, for each remembers only too well what was done and would, similarly circumstanced, do it again.

St. Paul long ago foretold Oceania: "There is not one just man. . . . All have gone astray together; they have become worthless. There is none who does good, no, not even one."[22] Paul, however, has a remedy where Orwell has none. Oceania's God is no redeemer but the guarantor of despair. Orwell feared the Superman and disbelieved in grace; the peculiar terror of *Nineteen Eighty-Four* is that it has no solution to the problem it propounds. O'Brien predicts Winston's future: "'We shall crush you down to the point from which there is no coming back. . . . Everything will be dead within you. Never again will you be capable of love, or friendship, or joy of living, or laughter, or curiosity, or courage, or integrity. You will be hollow. We shall squeeze you empty, and then we shall fill you with ourselves'" (p. 203). It is a promise devastatingly kept. The modern Gulliver is in far more desperate case than his alienated predecessor. At the close of Orwell's dark prophecy, the rout of humanism is total.

7

CONCLUSION

It would be easy—but wrong—to conclude that *Nineteen Eighty-Four* is a work of paralyzing pessimism. Certainly it is a work charged with despair so intense that some readers do react to it as to Medusa in the myth, but getting stoned is not what Orwell intended. The warning, we are told, defeats itself because of its boundless pessimism.[1] If the object is to help people resist totalitarianism, the utter ruin of the would-be rebel is hardly likely to strengthen their resolve. Behind such complaints lies a preference for the original movie version in which Winston dies like Leonidas at Thermopylae or Crockett in the Alamo, much as the eighteenth century favored Nahum Tate's *Lear* to Shakespeare's. I have already noted Orwell's definition of tragedy, and it is not unreasonable to ask why he refused to make his own contribution to the genre with his last book (*CEJL*, 4:338). It is the more puzzling when we recall his disapproval of quitters and power worshippers: "There is nothing for it but to die fighting, but one must above all die *fighting* and have the satisfaction of killing someone else first" (*CEJL*, 2:397). Why did he deny this satisfaction to Winston? "Giants stamping on pygmies is the characteristic pattern of our age."[2] Why did he make his own spectacular addition to the pattern he deplored? It is tempting but mistaken to seek an explanation in capitulation to despair.

Other critics deny that Orwell despairs.[3] Winston despairs so that we may be entertained. We are spectators of a humane comedy full of cleansing, mocking laughter—not the human condition in some dark, Swiftian sense but the follies of certain power-hungry delinquents is what the book is about. The final image of Winston, gazing infatuated at Big Brother with gin-stained tears running down his nose, is intended to make us smile, not shudder. Why on earth blame Orwell because people cannot read properly or lack a sense of humor? Is it his fault if we fail to see the joke? And yet so many readers *have* failed to see the joke that the advocates of the comic view are driven, finally, to rebuke Orwell himself: "Orwell was at best incautious, at worst foolish."[4] He should have known better than to leave his text so ambiguously open, so vulnerable to misinterpretation. Why didn't he make it unequivocally clear that he believed in a prole victory and explain why he did so? Why didn't he anticipate those charges about personal neurosis, mysticism of cruelty, and the rest and make it plain to all that he was writing a satire against the power hungry?[5] Yet many readers will be grateful that he did no such thing, for the book he wrote is a great book and the one he did not write is nothing. It is foolish to attack Orwell for alleged mysticism of cruelty when none of us, Deutscher included, can fully explain the mystery of totalitarianism. It is absurd to censure a writer for acknowledging with rare honesty his sense of helplessness before the "ultimate" meaning of totalitarianism—especially if he happens to have given us the most graphic vision of totalitarianism that has yet been composed. We should be grateful, not griping.

The truth is that neither of these views, paralyzing pessimism or comic satire, does justice to Orwell's masterpiece. The despair is present, is Orwell's, and is not enervating. Nor is this despair a regrettable inadvertence (Orwell imprudently saying more than he meant) or a shameful capitulation (Orwell deplorably saying more than he ought). This is deliberate, strategic despair, pondered, measured, which is meant to save, not stupefy, us. If some are stupefied, so much the worse for them. Orwell wants us to avoid Oceania and hopes we can do so—but not if we murmur "satire" as a charm to ward off evils. Oceania could happen unless we prevent it, and that we will scarcely do if we start from the comforting assumption that it is merely a bad dream. Who utters a warning against an impossibility? Who listens to it? Orwell clearly believed that the crystal spirit was in danger and urged its protection. His book is a conditional prophecy, a summons to preventive action, a tocsin to arouse his sleeping fellows. Those who tell us that the book is merely a comic exposé of one inadequate man or group of men, a satire on the power hungry that leaves the rest of us blameless and exonerated, who assure us that decency must triumph because the proles are invincible, those, in short, who sabotage the warning by neutering the threat, are, however unintentionally, frustrating the book's purpose. Cassandra is turned into an entertainer, the watchman into a wag; one might as sensibly remove the clapper from the tocsin.

Swift can be of service yet again. When Gulliver abandons us as incorrigible Yahoos, Swift does not want us to agree and continue equably in squalid Yahoodom. We are to be needled into proving Gulliver wrong by mending our ways. Our present condition is intolerable; can we reform, or are we past hope? Swift wants Gulliver to be wrong, though he fears that he is right. So too with Orwell. When his book concludes with the destruction of the human spirit, we are not to conclude that this is our fate, unavoidable and ordained. Neither, however, are we to smile at the absurdity of the supposition: it could happen unless we ensure that it does not. But hope and salvation are deliberately not within the text because Orwell means us to seek these in the street, not in the study. We are to earn them, not have them distributed to us as some kind of literary dole or handout. The text despairs so that we will not presume. Like those Hebrew prophets to whom he only half-facetiously compares himself, Orwell predicts calamity unless we repent (*CEJL*, 1:164).

This despair extends textually, as it must, to the proles. If there is hope, it is in the proles. But there is not. The proles are hopeless. That is the inescapable textual conclusion, though Orwell paradoxically goes on hoping that those defeated in fiction may triumph in fact. The time is surely long past for recognizing that *Nineteen Eighty-Four* is a work of fiction and not a politicosociological essay. Only then will commentators stop meddling, often for the noblest motives, with Orwell's creation. To go on intoning against the text that the proles are insuperable is to repeat the error that Orwell himself censured in Bertrand Russell as spokesman for liberalism: it is to confuse a prayer with an axiom, to adulterate judgment with desire (*CEJL*, 1:414). Of course, Orwell believed in the decency of ordinary people far more than he did in the integrity of intellectuals, and he continued to hope in the darkest times that this decency would prevail against the worst that totalitarianism might do. But there were, indisputably, times, too, when he feared it might not (*CEJL*, 3:122). The action of *Nineteen Eighty-Four* does nothing to confirm this faith in democratic invincibility; we can dream of a prole victory if we wish, but there is nothing in the text to justify, and much to discredit, it.

Orwell declines, within the text, to foster the assumption that the proles are insuperable, precisely because such slovenly trust, in attenuating his warning, will make Oceania more probable. Whatever he may believe externally, internally he denies to everyone, himself included, this consolation. It is this harshness toward his own cherished beliefs that has evoked deserved tributes to the celebrated honesty.[6] Orwell is not the shop for consolation; he will not promote wishes to facts or believe things because they are pleasant. And always the first victim of this severity is himself. The fact that Orwell wanted a prole victory is the guarantee that it will not be textually present.

Oceania will be avoided only if we take the threat seriously, and we are all of us, proles included, under threat. The intellectuals, so easily seducible by power, are more at risk, but no one is safe. The peculiarity of Orwell's book is that if it succeeds, it simultaneously fails; the better it is understood and the more urgently it is heeded, the lesser is the threat—in that case we should surely know whom to thank. If Oceania comes, *Nineteen Eighty-Four* will disappear down a memory hole; if Orwell is right, he will not be read. If Oceania does not come, the book will be read but by a growing number who find there merely a private nightmare, the manifestation of some psychic wound in its creator. If Orwell is wrong, he will be disparaged.

Yet Orwell wrote to make himself wrong: even in the act of utterance, this prophecy seeks to falsify itself. *Nineteen Eighty-Four* presents the basic Orwellian conflict, hope versus apprehension, in its most agonizing form. Anxious for the crystal spirit, Orwell hopes he is wrong; even in expressing his fears, he provokes us into proving them bugaboos. The book is unique in willing its own irrelevance and working for its own redundancy. Orwell never elected art above life, and the despairing art of *Nineteen Eighty-Four* was not intended to deflect us from the struggle to be human. But neither can the prophet hold his mouth on the edge of disaster.

We do Orwell a disservice in one of two equally fallacious ways. One is to see the undoubted despair and conclude that Orwell follows his text in surrendering to it; the other is to deny that there is any despair present to tempt either Orwell or ourselves. But Orwell neither quits nor placates; *Nineteen Eighty-Four* paradoxically continues to fight for man even as it depicts the destruction of the last man alive. Winston is doomed, and man with him, but we are not yet Winston, and, even in the pit of its pessimism, *Nineteen Eighty-Four* exhorts us not to become so. The text is summoning us to a struggle that is not yet lost. It is we, here and now, who will decide that outcome: Winston's future fate depends upon our present action.

This is, after all, the essence of the Judeo-Christian tradition of prophecy: it is always conditional, forever tied to human deeds and choices. If you eat this apple, you will lose Eden; if you battle onward, you will reach the Promised Land; if you do what is just, you will be saved. Otherwise, no. It all depends on you, your choosing, your doing. The woe foretold by the prophet will descend unless people change their ways: Nineveh, the great city, will be destroyed unless Jonah acts, and Nineveh listens. Orwell is the last of the prophets, the Jonah sent to us, and we would do well, as Nineveh did, to listen and repent.

Scrooge, carried to a churchyard by the Ghost of Christmas Yet to Come and motioned toward a grave, implores an answer to one question: "'Are these the shadows of the things that Will be, or are they the shadows of things that May be, only?'" Scrooge concedes that certain courses of human action persevered in must produce certain results but begs to be told that "'If the courses be departed from, the ends will change.'"[7] It is the question that we inevitably put to *Nineteen Eighty-Four*, demanding of Orwell the nature of the shadows, ineluctable or contingent, cast by his dark book: is Oceania a fate or a warning? What will happen or what may, a solicitation to despair or a call to action? Satan in hell attempts to recruit the demoralized angels: "Awake, arise, or be for ever fallen!"—in vain, because hell is too late to recover.[8] Oceania too is hell, but we are not yet in it, and Orwell employs Satan's summons to ensure that we never will be. Scrooge's question is answered: it is up to you.

Orwell is in our time the chief custodian of this tradition of human responsibility and moral choice. True, *Nineteen Eighty-Four* is "the last great book he happened to write before he happened to die."[9] Yet it is also a kind of testament, however unwitting, the finely appropriate crown to a life of unremitting moral effort. Orwell dreamed of writing other books, and we mourn that he was not spared to do so. Yet, paradoxically, rather than a sense of loss there is a sense of completion, of a hero dead yet with his triumphs secured:

> Samson hath quit himself
> Like Samson, and heroicly hath finished
> A life heroic.[10]

Nothing is here for tears. Of course, his last book is profoundly disturbing in that it demolishes our ignorance and our alibi together. We now know that we are responsible, and the closer Oceania comes, the guiltier we are. But this book of destruction can also be our means of salvation, and if we do save ourselves, we should remember our chief benefactor. Without minimizing the threat or underestimating the danger, we must believe (but not too easily) that we can foil Oceania. That is the human response and is surely the one that Orwell sought. When we are finally safe, we should do homage for our deliverance to this fiercest tocsin of the twentieth century; it would be a shabby re-compense if future generations, untroubled in their freedom, were to find in *Nineteen Eighty-Four* only the hysteria of a neurotic panic-monger, ungratefully unaware of the unbreakable nexus between their freedom and this book.[11]

NOTES

Chapter 1

1. George Orwell, *The Collected Essays, Journalism and Letters*, ed. Sonia Orwell and Ian Angus (hereafter cited parenthetically in the text as *CEJL*). (Harmondsworth, Middlesex: Penguin, 1970), 1:28.

2. George Orwell, *Homage to Catalonia*, (Harmondsworth, Middlesex: Penguin, 1962), pp. 144–72; *CEJL*, 1:29.

3. Bernard Crick, *George Orwell: A Life*, (London: Secker and Warburg, 1950), p. 386.

4. T. S. Eliot, "Tradition and the Individual Talent," in *The Sacred Wood: Essays on Poetry and Criticism* (London and New York: Methuen, 1986), pp. 47–59.

5. Ibid., p. 49.

6. George Orwell, *Nineteen Eighty-Four* (Harmondsworth, Middlesex: Penguin, 1954), p. 134 (hereafter cited parenthetically in the text).

7. Jenni Calder, *"Animal Farm" and "Nineteen Eighty-Four"* (Philadelphia: Open University Press, 1987), pp. 23–25.

8. William Steinhoff, *George Orwell and the Origins of "1984"* (Ann Arbor: University of Michigan Press, 1975).

9. Edward M. Thomas, *Orwell* (Edinburgh: Oliver and Boyd, 1965), p. 3.

Chapter 2

1. Julien Benda, *The Betrayal of the Intellectuals*, trans. Richard Aldington (Boston: Beacon Press, 1959).

2. Crick, *George Orwell*, p. xx.

3. Norman Podhoretz, "If Orwell Were Alive Today," *Harper's* 266 (January 1983), in *Twentieth-Century Literary Criticism*, ed. Dennis Poupard

and James E. Person, Jr. (Detroit: Gale Research Company, 1985), pp. 333–37.

4. See Jeffrey Meyers, *A Reader's Guide to George Orwell* (London, Thames and Hudson, 1975), p. 58.

5. Horace *Satires*, 1.1.69–70 (*Mutato nomine de te / fabula narratur*: "change the name and the story is told about you"). 2 Samuel 12:7

6. Philip Rahv, quoted in Crick, *George Orwell* p. 397.

7. John H. Barnsley, "The Last Man in Europe: A Comment on George Orwell's *1984*," *Contemporary Review* V 239 (July 1981), in *Twentieth-Century Literary Criticism*, p. 324.

8. Lawrence Malkin, "Halfway to *1984*," *Horizon* 12 (Spring 1970), in *Twentieth-Century Literary Criticism*, p. 296.

9. See Patrick Reilly, *George Orwell: The Age's Adversary* (New York: St. Martin's Press, 1986), pp. 59–93.

10. Edmund Burke, *Reflections on the Revolution in France*, ed. Conor Cruise O'Brien (Harmondsworth, Middlesex: Penguin, 1969), p. 90.

Chapter 3

1. Crick, *George Orwell*, p. 393; Jeffrey Meyers, ed., *George Orwell: The Critical Heritage* (London: Routledge and Kegan Paul, 1975), pp. 253, 256.

2. Crick, *George Orwell*, p. 393.

3. Ibid., p. 394. See also Meyers, *Orwell*, pp. 274–76, 282–83, 287–93.

4. Crick, *George Orwell*, p. 393; Meyers, *Orwell*, pp. 280–81.

5. Crick, *George Orwell*, p. 394

6. Ibid., p. 396; Meyers, *Orwell*, pp. 247, 248.

7. *Dr. Johnson on Shakespeare*, ed. W. K. Wimsatt (Harmondsworth, Middlesex: Penguin, 1969), p. 126; Crick, *George Orwell*, p. 396; Meyers, *Orwell*, p. 250.

8. *Horace Walpole's Correspondence with the Countess of Upper Ossorry*, V 32 ed. W. S. Lewis and A. Dayle Wallace with the assistance of Edwine M. Martz (London: Oxford University Press; New Haven: Yale University Press, 1965), p. 315.

9. George Orwell, *Nineteen Eighty-Four*, critical introduction and annotations by Bernard Crick (Oxford: Clarendon Press, 1984), pp. 15, 55.

10. Crick, *George Orwell*, p. 397.

11. Ibid., p. 399.

12. Meyers, *Orwell*, p. 290.

13. Isaac Deutscher in Raymond Williams, ed., *George Orwell: A Col-*

lection of Critical Essays (Englewood Cliffs, N.J.: Prentice-Hall, 1974), pp. 119–32.

14. Williams, *Orwell,* p. 126.

15. Ibid., p. 126.

16. Russell Kirk, "George Orwell's Despair," *Intercollegiate Review 5,* no. 1 (Fall 1968), in *Twentieth-Century Literary Criticism,* p. 310.

17. Podhoretz, "If Orwell Were Alive Today," p. 355.

18. Ibid., p. 334.

19. Gordon Beadle, "George Orwell and the Neoconservatives," *Dissent* (Winter 1984), in *Twentieth-Century Literary Criticism,* pp. 354–56. See also Robert Christgau in ibid., pp. 342–44.

20. Crick, *George Orwell,* p. 399.

21. Anthony West, *Principles and Persuasions* (London: Eyre and Spottiswoode, 1958).

22. Murray Sperber, "Gazing into the Glass Paperweight: The Structure and Psychology of Orwell's 1984," *Modern Fiction Studies* 26, no. 2 (Summer 1980), in *Twentieth-Century Literary Criticism,* p. 319.

23. Crick, *George Orwell,* p. 396.

24. Crick, ed., *Nineteen Eighty-Four,* p. 55.

25. André Brink, "Writing against Big Brother: Notes on Apocalyptic Fiction in South Africa," *World Literature Today* 58, no. 2 (Spring 1984), in *Twentieth-Century Literary Criticism,* p. 357.

26. Isaac Asimov, "Nineteen Eighty-Four" (from *Asimov on Science Fiction),* in *Twentieth-Century Literary Criticism,* p. 316.

27. George Orwell, *Coming Up for Air* (Harmondsworth, Middlesex: Penguin, 1962), p. 157 (hereafter cited parenthetically in the text).

Chapter 4

1. Jonathan Swift, *Gulliver's Travels,* ed. Peter Dixon and John Chalker with an Introduction by Michael Foot (Harmondsworth, Middlesex: Penguin, 1987), p. 65.

2. Joseph Conrad, *Heart of Darkness,* ed. Paul O'Prey (Harmondsworth, Middlesex: Penguin, 1983), pp. 46–47.

3. John Milton, *Paradise Lost,* ed Alastair Fowler (London: Longman, 1971), p. 91.

4. Jonathan Swift, *Gulliver's Travels,* op. cit., pp. 286, 294.

5. He wrote, "To be brought up to date it should be called Jack the Dwarf-Killer" (*CEJL,* 3:258). See also George Orwell, *The Lion and the Unicorn* (Harmondsworth, Middlesex: Penguin, 1982), p. 41; Reilly, *Orwell,* pp. 87–88.

6. *Othello*, act 5, sc. 2, line 300.

7. West, *Principles and Persuasions*. See also D. S. Savage, "The Fatalism of George Orwell," in *The New Pelican Guide to English Literature*, ed. Boris Ford, vol. 8: *The Present* (Harmondsworth, Middlesex: Penguin, 1983), p. 143.

8. John Atkins, "Orwell in 1984," *College Literature* 11, no. 1, (1984), in *Twentieth-Century Literary Criticism*, p. 354.

9. Nicoló Machiavelli, *The Prince*, trans. George Bull (Harmondsworth, Middlesex: Penguin, 1961), pp. 96–97. See also pp. 52, 59–60.

10. Friedrich Nietzsche, *The Birth of Tragedy and The Genealogy of Morals*, trans. Francis Golffing (Garden City, N.Y.: Doubleday, Anchor Books, 1956), p. 178.

11. *Measure for Measure*, act 2;, sc. 2, lines 107–9.

12. Raymond Aron, *Main Currents in Sociological Thought*, trans. Richard Howard and Helen Weaver (Harmondsworth, Middlesex: Penguin, 1970), pp. 159–64. See also Robert Michels, *Political Parties: A Sociological Study of the Oligarchical Tendencies in Modern Society* (Glencoe, Ill.: Free Press, 1958), *CEJL*, 4:211.

13. Brink, "Writing against Big Brother," p. 357. See also Machiavelli, *The Prince*, p. 117.

Chapter 5

1. Milton, *Paradise Lost*, p. 240.

2. Ibid., p. 59.

3. Charles Dickens, *Oliver Twist*, ed. Peter Fairclough (Harmondsworth, Middlesex: Penguin, 1966), pp. 461–62.

4. Lord Byron, *Don Juan*, ed. T. G. Steffan, E. Steffan, and W. W. Pratt (Harmondsworth, Middlesex: Penguin, 1977), p. 94.

5. Milton, *Paradise Lost*, p. 490.

6. Ibid., p. 494.

7. Ibid., p. 452.

8. Ibid., pp. 224–25.

9. Burke, *Reflections*, p. 200.

10. Jonathan Swift, *The Complete Poems*, ed. Pat Rogers (Harmondsworth, Middlesex: Penguin, 1983), pp. 448–52, 455–63.

11. T. S. Eliot, *The Complete Poems and Plays* (London: Faber and Faber, 1969), p. 86.

12. Milton, *Paradise Lost*, pp. 454–55.

13. Ibid., p. 221.

14. John Milton, "Areopagitica," in *Selected Prose*, ed. C. A. Patrides (Harmondsworth, Middlesex: Penguin, 1974), pp. 212–14.

15. Jonathan Swift, *A Tale of a Tub*, in *Selected Prose and Poetry*, ed. Edward Rosenheim, Jr. (New York: Rinehart and Winston, 1963), p. 122.

16. Ludwig Feuerbach, *The Essence of Christianity*, trans. George Eliot (New York, Harper Torchbooks, Harper & Row, 1957), p. 239.

17. Leszek Kolakowski, "The Priest and the Jester," in *Marxism and Beyond: On Historical Understanding and Individual Responsibility*, trans. Jane Zielonko Peel (London: Paladin, 1971), p. 31. See also Bryan Magee, *The Great Philosophers: An Introduction to Western Philosophy* (London: BBC Books, 1987), pp. 73–74.

18. Kolakowski, *Marxism and Beyond*, pp. 31–58; See Reilly, *Orwell*, pp. 81–93.

19. Crick, *George Orwell*, p. xx.

20. Milton, *Paradise Lost*, p. 190.

21. Christopher Marlowe, *Doctor Faustus*, ed. Roma Gill (London: Ernest Benn, and New York: W. W. Norton & Co., 1965), p. 19.

Chapter 6

1. E. M. Forster, *Two Cheers for Democracy* (Harmondsworth, Middlesex: London, 1974), p. 70.

2. Swift, *Gulliver's Travels*, pp. 223–37.

3. Ibid., p. 219.

4. Ibid., pp. 239–40.

5. Percy Bysshe Shelley, "The Mask of Anarchy," in *The Poetical Works of Shelley*, Selected with an Introduction by Morchard Bishop (London: Macdonald, 1949), p. 239.

6. George Orwell, *Keep the Aspidistra Flying* (Harmondsworth, Middlesex: Penguin, 1962), p. 255.

7. Swift, *Gulliver's Travels*, p. 173.

8. Ibid., pp. 223–24.

9. Ibid., pp. 252–60.

10. *The Correspondence of Jonathan Swift*, ed. Harold Williams (Oxford: Clarendon Press, 1963), 3:118.

11. *As You Like It*, act 3, sc. 2, lines 259–60.

12. Burke, *Reflections*, p. 135.

13. *William Blake: The Complete Poems*, ed. Alicia Ostriker (Harmondsworth, Middlesex: Penguin, 1977), p. 184.

14. R. S. Crane, "The Houyhnhnms, the Yahoos, and the History of

Ideas," in *Reason and the Imagination: Studies in the History of Ideas,* ed. J. A. Mazzeo (New York: Columbia University Press and London: Routledge and Kegan Paul, 1962), pp. 245–46.

15. *Milton: Complete Shorter Poems,* ed. John Carey (London: Longman, 1971), p. 209.

16. George Orwell, *Down and Out in Paris and London* (Harmondsworth, Middlesex: London, 1963), p. 147 (hereafter cited parenthetically in the text).

17. See Reilly, *Orwell,* p. 49.

18. Mikhail Yur'evich Lermontov, *A Hero of Our Time,* trans. Paul Foote (Harmondsworth, Middlesex: Penguin, 1966), pp. 19–20.

19. Albert Camus, *The Myth of Sisyphus,* trans. Justin O'Brien (Harmondsworth, Middlesex: Penguin, 1975), p. 42.

20. Swift, *Gulliver's Travels,* p. 241.

21. Ibid., p. 345.

22. Epistle to the Romans, 3:10–12.

Chapter 7

1. Deutscher, "The Mysticism of Cruelty," in Williams, *George Orwell: A Collection of Critical Essays,* p. 131; Savage, "The Fatalism of George Orwell," *New Pelican Guide to English Literature,* p. 143. G. S. Fraser, *The Modern Writer and His World* (Harmondsworth, Middlesex: Penguin, 1964), pp. 158–59.

2. Crick, ed., *Nineteen Eighty-Four,* p. 448.

3. Ibid., pp. 2, 3, 105.

4. Crick, *George Orwell,* p. 397.

5. Ibid., pp. 397–99.

6. Reilly, *Orwell,* pp. 30–58.

7. Charles Dickens, *The Christmas Books,* ed. Michael Slater (Harmondsworth, Middlesex: Penguin, 1971), 1:124.

8. Milton, *Paradise Lost,* p. 64.

9. Crick, *George Orwell,* p. 399.

10. *Milton: Complete Shorter Poems,* p. 398.

11. See Meyers, *A Reader's Guide to George Orwell,* p. 154; Richard Voorhees, *The Paradox of George Orwell* (Lafayette, Ind.: Purdue University Studies, 1961), pp. 27–37.

BIBLIOGRAPHY

Primary Works

Down and Out in Paris and London, 1933.

Burmese Days, 1934.

A Clergyman's Daughter, 1935.

Keep the Aspidistra Flying, 1936.

The Road to Wigan Pier, 1937.

Homage to Catalonia, 1938.

Coming Up for Air, 1939.

Inside the Whale, 1940.

The Lion and the Unicorn, 1941.

Animal Farm, 1945.

Critical Essays, 1946.

Nineteen Eighty-Four, 1949.

Collected Essays, Journalism and Letters of George Orwell. Edited by Sonia Orwell and Ian Angus. 4 vols. (All available in Penguin Books, Harmondsworth, Middlesex, 1970).

Editions of Nineteen Eighty-Four

Nineteen Eighty-Four. Harmondsworth, Middlesex: Penguin, 1954.

Nineteen Eighty-Four. With a Critical Introduction and Annotations by Bernard Crick. Oxford: Clarendon Press, 1984.

Nineteen Eighty-Four: The Facsimile of the Extant Manuscript. Edited by Peter Davidson. New York: Harcourt Brace Jovanovich, 1984.

Orwell's Nineteen Eighty-Four: Text, Sources, Criticism. Edited by Irving Howe. New York: Harcourt Brace Jovanovich, 1982. Includes essays by Lionel Trilling, Arthur Koestler and Hannah Arendt.

Nineteen Eighty-Four. Edited by Linda Cookson. Longman Study Texts. Glasgow: Longman, 1983.

Nineteen Eighty-Four. With an Introduction and Appreciation by Julian Symons. London: Heron Books, 1970.

Secondary Works

Books

Alldritt, Keith. *The Making of George Orwell.* London: Edward Arnold, 1969. Scholarly investigation of Orwell's development as a writer, showing him as rebelling against the symbolist assumptions of his time.

Atkins, John. *George Orwell.* New York: Frederick Ungar, 1965. Basic survey of Orwell's work written from the viewpoint of friend rather than literary critic, celebrating Orwell's decency.

Brander, Lawrence. *George Orwell.* London: Longmans, 1954. Basic survey of Orwell's work written from the viewpoint of friend rather than literary critic; assumes too easily an autobiographical element in the works.

Burgess, Anthony. *1985.* London: Arrow Books, 1980. A major living novelist uses his own dystopia to advance his critique of Orwell's book.

Calder, Jenni. *Chronicles of Conscience: A Study of George Orwell and Arthur Koestler.* London: Secker and Warburg, 1968. A comparative study of the whole body of work by both men, examining them as prophets and revolutionaries; this is the first study to see Orwell in a wider European perspective.

———. *Huxley and Orwell: "Brave New World" and "1984".* London: Edward Arnold, 1976. A comparative approach to the two outstanding dystopian novels of our century.

———. *"Animal Farm" and "Nineteen Eighty-Four".* Philadelphia and Milton Keynes: Open University Press, 1987. A critical analysis of Orwell's last two major works.

Chilton, Paul, and Aubrey, Crispin. *"Nineteen Eighty-Four" in 1984.* London: Comedia Publishing Group, 1983. Collection of essays on aspects of current social and political life resembling situations portrayed in Orwell's novel.

Crick, Bernard. *George Orwell: A Life.* London: Secker and Warburg, 1980; Middlesex: Penguin, Harmondsworth, 1982. The authorized biography, objective and unspeculative—the first biographer to be given access to private papers held by Orwell's widow.

Fyvel, T. R. *George Orwell: A Personal Memoir.* London: Macmillan, 1982. An account by a close friend upholding Orwell as a secular saint and arguing that in *Nineteen Eighty-Four,* out of his private nightmare he produced a book prophetically related to the public problems of the age.

Garrett, J. C. *Utopias in Literature.* New Zealand: University of Canterbury Press, 1968. Locates *Nineteen Eighty-Four* within the dystopian genre with Jack London, Zamiatin, and Aldous Huxley.

Gerber, Richard. *Utopian Fantasy: A Study of English Utopian Fiction since the End of the Nineteenth Century.* London: Routledge & Kegan Paul, 1955. *Nineteen Eighty-Four* is representative of the modern scientific utopia where man is drained of all individuality. Gerber attacks the book as too despairing.

Gross, Miriam, ed. *The World of George Orwell.* New York: Simon and Schuster, 1972. A number of brief biographies and critical essays that place Orwell's achievement in the context of his own period; the best essays are by William Empson and Malcolm Muggeridge.

Heppenstall, Rayner. *Four Absentees.* London: Barrie and Rockcliff, 1960. On the whole, hostile anecdotal reminiscences by an acquaintance who once shared a flat with Orwell in London: Orwell emerges as a prejudiced eccentric.

Hollis, Christopher. *A Study of George Orwell: The Man and His Works.* London: Hollis and Carter, 1956. A basic survey by a contemporary at Eton who met up with Orwell again in Burma. Hollis traces in Orwell a "revolt against revolt" and emphasizes his conservatism.

Hopkinson, Tom. *George Orwell.* London: Longman, Green, 1953. Competent survey of Orwell's life and work from the standpoint of a personal friend. Sees Orwell as preoccupied with the present, to the detriment of both past and future.

Howe, Irving. *"1984" Revisited: Totalitarianism in Our Century.* New York: Harper & Row, 1982. Argues that the book should be read as a mixture of genres: Menippean satire, conventional novel, tract, romance.

Hunter, Lynette. *George Orwell: The Search for a Voice.* Stony Stratford, England: Open University Press, 1984. Examines Orwell's narrative voice in his major works.

Hynes, Samuel, ed. *Twentieth Century Interpretations of "1984": A Collection of Critical Essays.* Englewood Cliffs, N.J.: Prentice-Hall, 1971. A valuable collection of critical essays and reviews. Hynes finds in Orwell a tension between the need for political action and the desire for a private life.

Jensen, Ejner J., ed. *The Future of "Nineteen Eighty-Four."* Ann Arbor:

University of Michigan Press, 1984. Collection of critical essays on the relevance of the book, published in the year of its title.

Kalechofsky, Roberta. *George Orwell.* New York: Frederick Ungar, 1973. Simplified discussion of the major works.

Kubal, David. *Outside the Whale: George Orwell's Art and Politics.* Notre Dame, Ind.: Notre Dame University Press, 1972. Reads *Nineteen Eighty-Four* as a deterministic prophecy.

Lee, Robert A. *Orwell's Fiction.* Notre Dame: University of Notre Dame Press, 1968. Shifts the emphasis away from fictionalized autobiography and social criticism to the books as fiction. Finds the major theme to be the failure and corruption of language.

Leif, Ruth Ann. *Homage to Oceania: The Prophetic Vision of George Orwell.* Columbus: Ohio State University Press, 1969. Study of Orwell's political beliefs as evinced in his work, upholding his humanism and belief in the ordinary man.

Leyburn, Ellen Douglass. *Satiric Allegory: A Mirror for Man.* New Haven: Yale University Press, 1956. A survey of the satiric tradition in English, including Swift and Orwell. Finds *Nineteen Eighty-Four* defective as an allegory.

Meyers, Jeffrey, ed. *George Orwell: The Critical Heritage.* London: Routledge and Kegan Paul, 1975. Important collection of reviews and critical essays with a useful introduction.

———. *A Reader's Guide to George Orwell.* London: Thames and Hudson, 1975. A valuable chronological survey of Orwell's work with a useful concluding chapter on the critics.

Milosz, Czeslaw. *The Captive Mind.* New York: Alfred A. Knopf, 1953. Praises Orwell for his insight into the concentration camp society and is amazed that a writer who never lived in Russia should have such a keen perception into its life.

Oxley, B. *George Orwell.* London: Evans Brothers, 1967. Introductory study of the genre of Orwell's work, concluding that he is best understood as a pamphleteer, a journalist responding to political events.

Poupard, Dennis, and Person, James E.,, eds. "Orwell" in *Twentieth-Century Literature Criticism,* vol. 15. Detroit: Gale Research Co., 1985. Important collection of critical reviews and essays from the earliest notices until 1984.

Rees, Richard. *George Orwell: Fugitive from the Camp of Victory.* London: Secker and Warburg, 1961. Comprehensive study of Orwell as a man rather than a literary figure written by a close friend. Traces four elements in Orwell: rebel, traditionalist, rationalist, romantic.

Reilly, Patrick. *George Orwell: The Age's Adversary.* London: Macmillan; New York, St. Martin's Press, 1986. A critical analysis of all of Orwell's works.

Bibliography

Sandison, Alan. *The Last Man in Europe.* London: Macmillan, 1974. Locates Orwell within the tradition of heroic Protestant nonconformity.

Small, Christopher. *The Road to Miniluv: George Orwell, the State and God.* London: Gollancz, 1975. Uncovers the underlying religious problem in Orwell's book, arguing that Orwell's anguish comes from recognizing that "if God is a myth, socialised humanity is just as much so."

Smyer, Richard I. *Primal Dream and Primal Curse: Orwell's Development as a Psychological Novelist.* Columbia: University of Missouri Press, 1979. Discusses Orwell's novels as manifestations of sexual guilt.

Stansky, Peter, ed. *On "Nineteen Eighty-Four."* San Francisco: W. H. Freeman, 1983. A collection of essays to commemorate the date of the novel.

Stansky, Peter, and Abrahams, William. *The Unknown Orwell.* New York: Alfred A. Knopf, 1972. Biography of Orwell's first thirty years.

———. *Orwell: The Transformation.* New York: Alfred A. Knopf, 1980. Biography from the publication of his first novel to his involvement in the Spanish Civil War.

Steinhoff, William. *George Orwell and the Origins of "1984."* Ann Arbor: University of Michigan Press, 1975. Presents the text as the culminating development of Orwell's political beliefs, expressing a lifetime's attitudes and ideas.

Thomas, Edward. *Orwell.* Edinburgh: Oliver and Boyd, 1965. Introductory survey suggesting that the Orwell we meet in the works may be a consciously contrived literary persona. Orwell's chief theme is a betrayal of the clerks and a capitulation to power.

Voorhees, Richard. *The Paradox of George Orwell.* Lafayette, Ind.; Purdue University Studies, 1961. The first scholarly study not by an acquaintance, analyzing Orwell's paradoxical attitudes to rebellion, power, and socialism.

Warburg, Frederic. *All Authors Are Equal.* London: Hutchinson, 1973. Personal reminiscences by the publisher of *Nineteen Eighty-Four* and *Animal Farm,* providing valuable information about the publishing background.

Wilding, Michael. *Political Fictions.* London: Routledge and Kegan Paul, 1980. Analyzes *Nineteen Eighty-Four* within a tradition of political fiction including *News from Nowhere, The Iron Heel, The Rainbow, Kangaroo* and *Darkness at Noon.* Orwell exhibits a hostility to the progressive, all the more virulent because of his own sense of impotence.

Williams, Raymond. *Orwell.* With Afterword. London: Fontana Books, 1984. Criticizes Orwell from a Marxist viewpoint for his "radical pessimism" and "accommodation to capitalism."

———. *George Orwell: A Collection of Critical Essays.* Englewood Cliffs, N.J.: Prentice-Hall, 1974. Covers the major aspects of Orwell's work with some of the essays sharing Williams's Marxist approach.

Winnifreth, Tom, and Whitehead, William V. *"1984" and All's Well?* London: Macmillan, 1984. Examines some aspects of modern popular culture in the light of *Nineteen Eighty-Four.*

Woodcock, George. *The Crystal Spirit: A Study of George Orwell.* Boston: Little, Brown, 1966. One of the best general studies written by a friend providing the fullest biographical discussion of the man, as well as an explication of his fiction, criticism, and political ideas.

Zwerdling, Alec. *Orwell and the Left.* New Haven: Yale University Press, 1974. An excellent defense of the position that Orwell was "an internal critic of socialism," not a defector from it. Presents Orwell as a diagnostician of the Left's ills.

Articles and Chapters of Books

Allen, Francis A. *"Nineteen Eighty-Four* and the Eclipse of the Private World." *Michigan Quarterly Review* 12 no. 4 (Fall 1983). Argues that the individual's loss of privacy is the most frightening aspect of Orwell's dystopia.

Ashe, Geoffrey. "Second Thoughts on *Nineteen Eighty-Four,*" *Month,* n.s. 4, no. 5 (November 1950). Interprets the book as an attack on left-wing progressive thought but sees it primarily as a horror story.

Asimov, Isaac. *"Nineteen Eighty-Four."* In *Asimov on Science Fiction.* Garden City, N.Y.: Doubleday, 1981. Sees the book as a denunciation of Stalinism, but a failure as either prophecy or science fiction.

Auden, W. H. "George Orwell." *Spectator,* 16 January 1971. Praises Orwell as a vigorous and lucid writer whose one blind spot was an essentially religious hatred of Christianity.

Barnsley, John H. "The Last Man in Europe: A Comment on George Orwell's *1984."* *Contemporary Review,* 239, no. 1386 (July 1981). Quarrels with Orwell's pessimistic view of the proles and with his view of technology as a means of repression.

Barr, Alan. "The Paradise Behind *1984."* In *English Miscellany: A Symposium of History, Literature and the Arts.* Edited by Mario Praz. Rome: British Council, 1968. Examines some religious parallels and allusions in the text.

Baruch, Elaine Hoffman. "The Golden Country: Sex and Love in *1984."* In *"1984" Revisited: Totalitarianism in Our Century.* Edited by Irving Howe. New York: Harper & Row, 1982. Finds in the novel a "romanticisation of the domestic" that explains the negative reaction of feminist reviewers of the novel.

Beadle, Gordon. "George Orwell and the Death of God." *Colorado Quarterly* 23 (1974). Explores Orwell's conviction that it is impossible to believe in

God yet imperative to behave morally. *Nineteen Eighty-Four* is a warning of where loss of belief might lead.

———. "George Orwell and the Neoconservatives." *Dissent* (Winter 1984). Challenges the appropriation of Orwell by the neoconservatives.

Beauchamp, Gorman. "Of Man's Last Disobedience: Zamiatin's *We* and Orwell's *1984.*" *Comparative Literature Studies* 10, no. 4 (December 1973). Identifies Adam in the religious myth as the ancestor of Orwell's rebel.

———. "From Bingo to Big Brother: Orwell on Power and Sadism." In *The Future of "Nineteen Eighty-Four."* Edited by Ejner J. Jensen. Ann Arbor: University of Michigan Press, 1984. Finds a link between Oceania and the harsh boarding-school that Orwell attended as a boy.

Bell, Daniel. "1984." *New Leader,* 25 June 1949. Sees the book as "a morality play which preaches the absolute truth that man is an end in himself" but which also shows that, exposed to absolute power, "the human being becomes completely malleable."

Birrell, T. A. "Is Integrity Enough? A Study of George Orwell." *Dublin Review* 224 (Autumn 1950). The novel reveals the spiritual bankruptcy of integrity that is divorced from supernatural belief.

Brink, André. "Writing against Big Brother: Notes on Apocalyptic Fiction in South Africa." *World Literature Today* 58, no. 2 (Spring 1984). Relates Orwell's novel to the contemporary situation in South Africa but argues that Orwell is finally an optimist.

Burns, Wayne. "George Orwell: Our "Responsible" Quixote." *West Coast Review,* 1967. Sees the novel as Orwell's departure from his previous work in which he shows the emptiness of the values he had formerly defended.

Byrne, Katherine. "George Orwell and the American Character." *Commonweal,* 12 April 1974. A summary of Orwell's attitude to America, deploring, among other things, the cult of power in pulp fiction.

Calder, Jenni. "Orwell's Post-War Prophecy." In *George Orwell: A Collection of Critical Essays.* Edited by Raymond Williams. Englewood Cliffs, N.J.: Prentice-Hall, 1974. Relates the book to the intensity with which Orwell reacted against both the conditions of postwar Britain and the deadlock of the international situation.

Chatfield, Jack. "Orwell's Achievement." *National Review,* 29 August 1975. Finds Orwell's influence as great among the masses as among the intellectuals. The language and atmosphere of *Nineteen Eighty-Four* are now part of our mental lives.

Christgau, Robert. "Writing for the People." *Village Voice,* 1983. Sees the Party's desire for power for its own sake as the most terrifying aspect of the novel.

College Literature. 11, no. 1 (1984). Issue devoted to studies of *Nineteen Eighty-Four.*

Colquitt, Betsy Feagan. "Orwell: Traditionalist in Wonderland." *Discourse* 8, (1965). *Nineteen Eighty-Four* expresses Orwell's fears that traditional values may be destroyed.

Connors, James. "Zamiatin's *We* and the Genesis of *1984*." *Modern Fiction Studies* 21 (1975). Argues against Isaac Deutscher that the influence of *We* upon *Nineteen Eighty-Four* has been greatly exaggerated.

———. "Do It to Julia: Thoughts on Orwell's *1984*." *Modern Fiction Studies* 16, no. 4 (Winter 1970–1971). Detects in the book a collapse of the previously healthy tension in Orwell between fear and hope but declines to accept Winston as the human representative.

Cronkite, Walter. Preface to *Nineteen Eighty-Four*. New York: New American Library, 1984. Stresses that the novel is a satirical warning and not a prophecy.

Deutscher, Isaac. "1984: The Mysticism of Cruelty." In *George Orwell: A Collection of Critical Essays*. Edited by Raymond Williams. Englewood Cliffs, N.J.: Prentice-Hall, 1974. A seminal essay attacking Orwell for delivering a warning that defeats itself because of its underlying boundless despair.

De Camara, Robert C. "Homage to Orwell." *National Review*, 13 May 1983. Finds in the book Orwell's abandonment of socialism in the terrible vision of a world after the triumph of socialism.

Dooley, D. J. "The Limitations of George Orwell." *University of Toronto Quarterly* 38 (1959). Believes that Orwell is limited by a predisposition to view everything pessimistically.

———. "The Freudian Critics of *1984*." *Triumph* 1 (1974). Rejects the Freudian interpretation by insisting that Orwell's fears are based on observed realities, not neurotic fancies.

Dyson, A. E. "Orwell: Irony as Prophecy." In *The Crazy Fabric: Essays in Irony*. London: Macmillan, 1965. Relates Orwell to Jonathan Swift, using Orwell's essay on Swift as evidence.

Edrich, Emanuel. "George Orwell and the Satire in Horror." *Texas Studies in Language and Literature* 4 (1962). Argues that Orwell is essentially a satirist who introduces horror into the beast fable and utopian novel.

Elbstree, Langdon. "The Structured Nightmare of *1984*." *Twentieth Century Literature* 5, no. 3 (October 1959). Contrasts Oceania, a world based on dreams and nightmares, with the world of objective reality.

Esslin, Martin. "Television and Telescreen." In *On 'Nineteen Eighty-Four.'* Edited by Peter Stansky. San Francisco: W. H. Freeman & Co., 1983. Locates the most terrifying aspect of the book in the developed power of the media to manipulate people.

Feder, Lillian. "Selfhood, Language and Reality: George Orwell's *Nineteen Eighty-Four*." *Georgia Review* 37, no. 2 (Summer 1983). Identifies the gravest threat of Oceania as the separation of language from any real referential function.

Fialka, John J. "The Time Has Come for Deciding If *1984* Will Resemble 1984." *Wall Street Journal,* 7 June 1983. Surveys some contemporary receptions of the book.

Forster, E. M. "George Orwell." In *Two Cheers for Democracy,* New York: Harvest, 1951. Vindicates Orwell by finding in our present world confirmation of his dark prophecies.

Fromm, Erich. Afterword to *Nineteen Eighty-Four.* New York: New American Library, 1983. Places the book in the dystopian tradition with Huxley's *Brave New World* and Zamiatin's *We.*

Geering, R. G. "*Darkness at Noon* and *Nineteen Eighty-Four*: A Comparative Study." *Australian Quarterly* 30, no. 3 (September 1958). Compares Koestler's fictionalized account of the Moscow purges with Orwell's Oceanic equivalent.

Gleckner, Robert. "1984 or 1948?" *College English* 18 (November 1956). The book should not be read as science fiction or as a criticism of the Soviet Union but as an attack on the general tendency to obliterate individuality and objective truth.

Godley, Chris. "The Abyss of Pessimism." *Granta,* 25 April 1964. Orwell pessimistically records the breakup of liberal-Christian culture and the emergence of a tightly organized society hostile to the writer.

Gray, Paul. "That Year Is Almost Here." *Time,* 28 November 1983. Emphasizes the great impact of the book on American popular culture.

Greenblatt, Stephen Jay. "George Orwell." In *Three Modern Satirists: Waugh, Orwell and Huxley.* New Haven: Yale University Press, 1965. Examines Orwell as a satirist, especially through an analysis of the disillusion of the 1940s as reflected in his novels; as he lost hope of radical change in society, he became pessimistic.

Hamilton, Kenneth M. "G. K. Chesterton and George Orwell: A Contrast in Prophecy." *Dalhousie Review* 31, no. 3 (Autumn 1951). Finds *Nineteen Eighty-Four* superior to *The Napoleon of Notting Hill* because of its greater realism.

Harris, Roy. "The Misunderstanding of Newspeak." *Times Literary Supplement,* 6 January 1984. Analyzes Orwell's fears that language could be used to obscure or pervert reality.

Hitchens, Christopher and Podhoretz, Norman. "An Exchange on Orwell." *Harper's* 266, no. 1593 (February 1983). A debate about Orwell's political attitudes.

Hobbs, Albert. "Welfarism and Orwell's Reversal." *Intercollegiate Review* 6 (1970). Uses Orwell to attack "socialistic" legislation in Britain and America since the 1930s.

Homberger, Eric. "A Social Theology: On Orwell." *Encounter* 43 (July 1974). Rejects Alan Sandison's view of Orwell's "religious" affinities to define him as a socialist and humanist.

Howe, Irving. "Orwell: History as Nightmare." In *Politics and the Novel*. Greenwich, Conn.: Fawcett, 1957. Sees the book as a unique literary attempt to create a world devoid of individualism, thereby answering Julian Symons's criticism concerning characterization. (See Symons.)

Huxley, Aldous. "A Footnote about *1984*." *World Review* 16 (June 1950). Suggests that modern techniques of conditioning have made the systematic brutality of Oceania out of date and make the possibility of future dictatorship even more frightening.

Jones, Joseph. "Utopia as Dirge." *American Quarterly* 2 (1950). Compares Twain's *Connecticut Yankee* with *Brave New World* and *Nineteen Eighty-Four*; Twain believes in science and technology; Huxley and Orwell see them as a threat.

Kateb, George. "The Road to *1984*." *Political Science Quarterly* 81, no. 4 (December 1966). Provides a political explanation for Orwell's pessimism and concludes that Orwell sacrifices ordinary wisdom in order to achieve an intensity of wisdom.

Kazin, Alfred. "Not One of Us." *New York Review of Books*, 14 June 1984. Praises Orwell for revealing the core of our century's political hideousness.

Kendrick, Walter. "Newspeak Double-Think." *Village Voice*, 1 February 1983. Dismisses the book as merely a reflection of Orwell's middle-class phobias concerning the common people.

Kessler, Martin. "Power and the Perfect State: A Study in Disillusionment as Reflected in Orwell's *Nineteen Eighty-Four* and Huxley's *Brave New World*." *Political Science Quarterly* 72, no. 4 (December 1957). Argues that Huxley's hedonistic trap is a more probable future for humanity than Orwell's concentration camp.

King, Carlyle. "The Politics of George Orwell." *University of Toronto Quarterly* 26 (1956). Believes that Orwell's faith in socialism stems from his schoolday humiliations and his guilt about his police service in Burma.

Kirk, Russell. "George Orwell's Despair." *Intercollegiate Review* 5, no. 1 (Fall 1968). Argues that Orwell's misanthropy and despair flow from his rejection of religious hope.

Koestler, Arthur. "A Rebel's Progress to George Orwell's Death." In *The Trail of the Dinosaur*. London: Hutchinson, 1970. Praises Orwell for his moral example and also as the only writer of genius among the writers of social revolt between the two world wars.

Kornbluth, C. M. "The Failure of the Science Fiction Novel as Social Criticism." In *The Science Fiction Novel: Imagination and Social Criticism*. Edited by Basil Davenport, Richard A. Heinlein, C. M. Kornbluth, Alfred

Bester, and Robert Bloch. Chicago: Advent Publishers, 1959. Argues that the horrors of Oceania derive from Orwell's unhappy childhood and that the text has failed to prevent the evils it depicts.

Labedz, Leopold. "Will George Orwell Survive 1984? of Doublethink and Double-Talk, Body-Snatching and Other Silly Pranks." parts 1 and 2, *Encounter* 63, nos. 1, 2 (June 1984, July–August 1984). Examines Orwell's political attitudes, concluding that these, translated into the 1980s, would sit more easily with right-wing thought.

McCarthy, Mary. "The Writing on the Wall." In *The Writing on the Wall and Other Literary Essays*. Harmondsworth, Middlesex: Penguin, 1973. Sees Orwell as a conservative by temperament longing to return to some simpler form of life.

McNamara, James, and O'Keefe, Dennis J. "Waiting for *1984*: On Orwell and Evil." *Encounter* 59, no. 6 (December 1982). Regards the book as a moral treatise about the state of the world after the destruction of capitalism.

Maddison, Michael. "*1984*: A Burnhamite Fantasy?" *Political Quarterly* (January–March 1961). Interprets the book as a depiction of James Burnham's managerial revolution and the growth of power elites.

Malkin, Lawrence. "Halfway to *1984*." *Horizon* 12, no. 2 (Spring 1970). Points to the threat of individual freedom emanating from collectives of both Left and Right.

Mander, John. "Orwell in the Sixties." In *The Writer and Commitment*. London: Secker and Warburg, 1961. Examines the inherent contradictions in Orwell's political thinking.

Mann, Golo. "*1984*." *Frankfurter Rundschau*, 5 November 1949. Argues that the book is not just an attack on communism or the Soviet Union but on totalitarianism from any quarter.

Modern Fiction Studies 21, no. 1 (Spring 1975). Issue devoted to Orwell.

Munk, Erika. "Love Is Hate: Women and Sex in *1984*." *Village Voice*, 1 February 1983. A feminist attack on Orwell for his attitude toward women, including his alleged failure to address women's issues.

New, Melvyn. "Orwell and Antisemitism: Towards *1984*." *Modern Fiction Studies* 21 (1975). Sees the book as Orwell's attempt to alert people to the horrors of the Nazi concentration camps.

———. "*Ad Nauseam*: A Satiric Device in Huxley, Orwell and Waugh." *Satire Newsletter* 8, no. 1 (Fall 1970). Examines Orwell's use of nauseating images in the book as a means of impersonally expressing moral indignation.

Patai, Daphne. "Gamesmanship and Androcentrism in Orwell's *1984*." *Publications of the Modern Languages Association* 97, no. 5 (October 1982). Examines the Party's pursuit of power for its own sake in terms of games theory.

Podhoretz, Norman. "If Orwell Were Alive Today." *Harper's* 266, no. 1592 (January 1983). Attempts to conscript Orwell for contemporary conservatism, arguing that today Orwell would be on the Right.

Popkin, Henry. "Orwell the Edwardian." *Kenyon Review* 16 (1954). Orwell vainly tried to extend the Edwardian period into his own time; his pessimism results from his failure.

Pritchett, V. S. "George Orwell." *New Statesman and Nation* 28 January 1950. Obituary praising Orwell as a secular saint, the guilty conscience of the educated and privileged.

Quintana, Ricardo. "George Orwell: The Satiric Resolution." *Wisconsin Studies in Contemporary Literature* 2 (1961). In becoming a satirist in his later novels, Orwell adopted the positives of England and traditional values, helping him to resist a conviction of evil.

Quinton, Anthony. "Orwell." *Encounter* 44 (May 1975). Reviewing William Steinhoff, Quinton argues that Orwell was not directly influenced by earlier books; they merely confirmed his own fears about power elites and warring superpowers.

Rahv, Philip. "The Unfuture of Utopia." *Partisan Review* 16 July 1949. Hails the book as the best antidote to the totalitarian disease ever produced—a warning to the Left that the threat to liberty could come from any quarter.

Ranald, Ralph A. "George Orwell and the Mad World: The Anti-Universe of *1984*." *South Atlantic Quarterly* 66, no. 4 (Autumn 1967). Reads the book as a satire alerting us to the threat of totalitarianism.

Rankin, David. "Orwell's Intentions in *1984*." *English Language Notes* 12, no. 3 (March 1975). Examines the political reception of the book against Orwell's own stated intentions.

Read, Herbert. "*1984*." *World Review* 16 June 1950. Describes it as Orwell's greatest book, its power related to the author's illness.

Reilly, Patrick. "*Nineteen Eighty-Four*: The Failure of Humanism." *Critical Quarterly* 24, no. 3 (Autumn 1982). Argues that the book discredits humanism as a valid creed for modern times.

———. "*Nineteen Eighty-Four*: The Insufficient Self." In *The Literature of Guilt: From "Gulliver" to Golding*. London: Macmillan; Ames: University of Iowa Press, 1988. Shows the relationship of *Nineteen Eighty-Four* to *Gulliver's Travels*, especially in a shared awareness of failure and corruption.

Rieff, Philip. "George Orwell and the Post-Liberal Imagination." *Kenyon Review* 16 (1954). Sees Orwell's problem as connected with the exhaustion of the liberal-Christian civilization. He is a naturally pious man who could not believe in salvation and is unable to live in a world no longer liberal.

Bibliography

Roazen, Paul. "Orwell, Freud and *1984*." *Virginia Quarterly Review* 54, no. 4 (Autumn 1978). Compares the attitudes of Freud and Orwell, relating psychoanalysis to the political system of Oceania.

Rosenfield, Isaac. "Decency and Death." *Partisan Review* (May 1950). Describes Orwell as a radical in politics and a conservative in feeling.

Russell, Bertrand. "Symptoms of Orwell's *1984*." In *Portraits from Memory and Other Essays*. London: George Allen and Unwin, 1956. Warns against dismissing the book as a private neurosis and detects the symptoms of the sickness in our own society.

Sarris, Andrew. "Chronicles of a Decent Man: Why He Wrote." *Village Voice*, 1 February 1983. Surveys some recent critical approaches to Orwell's life, work, and politico-social attitudes.

Savage, D. S. "The Fatalism of George Orwell." In *The New Pelican Guide to English Literature*. Edited by Boris Ford. Vol. 8: *The Present*. (Harmondsworth, Middlesex: Penguin, 1983). Attacks Orwell as a writer who has been grossly overvalued because of his "luck" in producing "tracts for the times."

Simms, Valerie J. "A Reconsideration of Orwell's *1984*: The Moral Implications of Despair." *Ethics* (July 1974). Analyzes the moral issues in *Nineteen Eighty-Four*.

Smith, Marcus. "The Wall of Blackness: A Psychological Approach to *1984*." *Modern Fiction Studies* 14, no. 4 (Winter 1968–1969). Proposes Winston Smith as the victim of an oedipal psychological disorder.

Spender, Stephen. "Anti-Vision and Despair." In *The Creative Element*. London: H. Hamilton, 1953; New York: British Book Center, 1954. Orwell's despair comes from the collapse of his faith in the idea of human equality.

Sperber, Murray. "Gazing into the Glass Paperweight: The Structure and Psychology of Orwell's *1984*." *Modern Fiction Studies* 26, no. 2 (Summer 1980). Compares the book with Freud's studies of paranoia, focusing on Orwell's overriding interest in exploring the world of human persecution.

Stewart, Ralph. "Orwell's Waste Land." *International Fiction Review* 8, no. 2 (Summer 1981). Finds T. S. Eliot's poetry, especially *The Waste Land*, a direct influence on Orwell's book.

Stokes, Geoffrey. "The History of the Future." *Village Voice*, 1 February 1983. Traces the history of utopian and dystopian novels, identifying *Nineteen Eighty-Four* as marking the triumph of the pessimistic outlook.

Strachey, John. "The Strangled Cry." In *Twentieth Century Interpretations of "1984": A Collection of Critical Essays*. Edited by Samuel Hynes. Englewood Cliffs, N.J.: Prentice-Hall, 1971. Identifies the theme of the falsification of the past as crucial not only to the novel but to Orwell in general.

Symons, Julian. "Power and Corruption." *Times Literary Supplement*,

10 June 1949. Regards the book as a serious examination of power and corruption, marred by a somewhat "schoolboyish" sensationalism and a sacrifice of characterisation to ideas. (See Howe, "History as Nightmare.")

Thale, Jerome. "Orwell's Modest Proposal." *Critical Quarterly* 4 (1962). Not a political or prophetic novel but an allegory of our present state of life, barren and lacking in individual choice.

Thompson, E. P. "Inside Which Whale?" In *George Orwell: A Collection of Critical Essays*. Edited by Raymond Williams. Englewood Cliffs, N.J.: Prentice-Hall, 1974. A historical analysis of the kind of disillusion that Orwell articulated and promulgated.

Trilling, Diana. "*1984*." *Nation*, 25 June 1949. Notes Orwell's "ability, so rare among intellectuals of the Left, to place his own brand of idealism above the uses of political partisanship."

Trilling, Lionel. "George Orwell and the Politics of Truth." In *The Opposing Self*." New York: Viking Press, 1955. One of the most generous earlier assessments of Orwell as the honest man, the secular saint.

Wain, John. "George Orwell I and II." In *Essays on Literature and Ideas*. London: Macmillan, 1963. Considers Orwell less as novelist than as writer of polemic and champion of intellectual freedom, especially in his critical essays.

———. "Orwell and the Intelligentsia." *Encounter* 21 (December 1968). Finds Orwell distrusting intellectuals and fearing above all a *trahison des clercs*.

———. "From Diagnosis to Nightmare: Koestler and Orwell on the Totalitarian Mind." *Encounter* 61, no. 2 (September–October 1983). Demonstrates that the functioning of a society such as Orwell depicted in Oceania would be physically and psychologically impossible.

Walsh, James. "George Orwell." *Marxist Quarterly* 3 (1956). A British Communist attacks Orwell for his insulting portrait of the proles of Oceania and dismisses the book as capitalist propaganda and neurotic hatreds.

Watson, George. "Orwell and the Spectrum of European Politics." *Journal of European Studies* 1 (1971). Orwell questioned the goals of socialism, seeing in particular the contradiction between libertarianism and egalitarianism and preferring reform to revolution.

Watt, Ian. "Winston Smith: The Last Humanist." In *On Nineteen Eighty-Four*. Edited by Peter Stansky. San Francisco: W. H. Freeman, 1983. Sees Winston as the only person in the novel who upholds the intellectual and moral values that had prevailed in the West for two millenia.

Wedgwood, Veronica. "*1984*." *Time and Tide*, 11 June 1949. Sees the book as an extension of certain characteristics and tendencies of 1948 to create an imaginary, satirical world of *1984*.

West, Anthony. "George Orwell." In *Principles and Persuasions*. London: Eyre and Spottiswoode, 1958. Advances the theory that the book stems from Orwell's neuroses (the "hidden wound") and attributes it to his experiences at boarding school.

Woodcock, George. "George Orwell and the Living Word." *Queen's Quarterly* 91, no. 3 (Autumn 1984). Examines Orwell's ideas of good and bad language, concluding with a discussion of Newspeak.

World Review, n.s., nos. 11–16 (June 1950). Issue devoted to Orwell criticism.

Bibliographies

Meyers, Jeffrey, and Meyers, Valerie. *George Orwell: An Annotated Bibliography of Criticism*. Reference Library of the Humanities Series, no. 54. New York: Garland, 1975.

Workman, Gillian. "Orwell Criticism." *Ariel* (University of Calgary) 3, no. 1 (1972).

INDEX

Index

Index

Index

ABOUT THE AUTHOR

Patrick Reilly was born in Glasgow and was educated at the University of Glasgow and at Pembroke College, Oxford, where he earned his B.Litt. with a thesis on "Jonathan Swift and Seventeenth-Century Scepticism." After a year as a school teacher Reilly joined the staff of the English Department at the University of Glasgow as assistant lecturer and is now senior lecturer. His publications include *Jonathan Swift: The Brave Desponder* (Manchester University Press, 1982), *George Orwell: The Age's Adversary* (Macmillan, 1986), *The Literature of Guilt: From "Gulliver" to Golding* (Macmillan, University of Iowa Press, 1988), the last with separate chapters on Swift, Conrad, Thomas Mann, Orwell, Camus, and William Golding. He has also published articles on Orwell, Joyce, Scottish literature, and education and religion and has contributed to several books, including *Henry Fielding: Justice Observed*, edited by K. G. Simpson (Barnes and Noble, 1985), and *Modern Scottish Catholicism 1878–1978*, edited by David McRoberts (Burns, 1979), as well as to four volumes of anthologized literary criticism.